IN THE SHADOWS OF GIANTS

by Michael Bayouth

**Growing Up
In The Shadow Of The
Motion Picture Industry**

In The Shadows of Giants

Published by Palm Avenue Publishing
Printed in the United States of America

In The Shadows of Giants

By

Michael Bayouth

FOREWORD

Since this book is an amalgam of stories from my life, in which my father has played such an integral part, I found it only fitting to ask him for his thoughts. Here they are:

Several people have interviewed me and the one question they always ask is: "Would you change anything in your life?"

No. Nothing could ever take the place of my family, my two boys and the love I have for them. Yes, I've done many things that most people will never do: I rode with the Jesse James gang. We robbed trains, stagecoaches— just about everything. Oh yeah, I went to the moon as well. I was with Robin Hood in the Sherwood Forest. Boy, what a great time we had.

I think of the experience I had in India when I was hunting a tiger that had plagued a village. There he was, ten feet up on a rock. My heart was beating a hundred miles an hour. I got the tiger. I had such a thrill I couldn't even put it into words.

Then I found myself, while filming Hatari, riding in a Jeep as a two thousand pound rhino was trying to put its horn through my leg. I can't tell you how I felt when that shot was over. I was so relieved it was done.

And what did I get out of it? "That's a great shot, Ted." That's all I ask for and that's all you ever get doing stunts. Not a day goes by that I don't think about one of them. How could I ever live a different life? Some of the great places I've been, still in my memory: Germany, India, Paris, London, New Guinea and Africa. And some of the great actors and directors I've worked with: John Wayne, Clark Gable, Victor Mature, Rock Hudson, Jim Garner, Howard Hawks, John Ford and David Lean, to name a few. This is my life. I asked for it. I lived it and I loved it.

– Ted White

DEDICATION

There is one person in particular to whom I would like to dedicate this book. One person who kept all the insanity and ludicrous antics that transpired in my life in check—that steady, constant, reliable place in my world that allowed us all to wig-out and come back to find a warm home, a warm meal and a warm place in her heart. My mom. Thanks mom, for putting up with us and being such a saint. Thanks for understanding when it made no sense at all. Thanks for sewing my jeans and the amazing advice. Never was there a more caring, lively and beautiful woman, inside and out. Your star is the brightest in the sky and it still guides me when I'm lost. You'll always live on in my memory—a warm, soft, glowing love that makes me smile. Keep your hand on my shoulder while your loving spirit is being blown by great winds across the sky.

ACKNOWLEDGEMENTS

The main person who I'd like to pedestal in this section is a woman worthy of praise, Jeri Bayouth, my step-mom. Being the wife of a stuntman is one thing, but being the wife of a man who's led such an over-sized life as my father, is another. One would tend to think any such woman would fall into the abyss of such a large shadow. She does not. Jeri has been his mountain of wisdom, love and support. And never was there a mightier rock that could bring down the giant at any given time. She has remained at his side for many years and withstood the fiercest of storms life could hurl at us. I raise my glass to her to acknowledge a real giant.

Thanks to my dad, Ted White, aka Ted Bayouth, for the countless hours he spent retelling some of these stories and for handing down to me his storytelling talents. And Dad, thanks for spending time with me as a kid and all the great experiences. Since this book has a lot to do with both of us, I won't go on and on, but I do want to say thanks for listening to me and burning all those ants with gas. That was really cool. And lastly, I'd like my $10 bucks back that you charged me for that magic set.

I don't think I would, or could, have written this book at all if it wasn't for my significant other, Kim Klein. Kim has literally kept the wind beneath my wings during these writings. She has pushed me with a tender guiding hand and aptly kept the wheels from falling off the bus on many occasions. My confidence, as a writer, came from her and I can confidently say, nowhere else. I can never repay her for the confidence, love and support she has given me. I'm sure it will travel well beyond these pages. Thank you!

Thank you to my brother, Ted Bayouth, for the stories and your continued support during the writing of this book. Being a bit wilder than I was growing up, your stories lent for some fun memories. Sorry I shot you in the eye with my slingshot. (Don't worry, he can still see okay.)

Also, thank you to my children: Taylor, Chelsea & Ben for their continued support of this undertaking and their unwavering love.

I'd like to send out a major thank you to team member, writer, editor and proofreader, Deb Coman. She not only did the book's copy editing but has been an instrumental presence during its completion.

Thanks to Tanya Russell aka Cha Cha Sandoval McMahon, founder of the *United Stuntwomen's Association* for your undying support and ongoing encouragement. She has doubled for such greats as Natalie Wood, Debra Winger, Susan Anton and Olivia Newton-John. She's worked with the likes of Clint Eastwood and Steven Spielberg and appeared in *CHiPs, Dukes of Hazzard, Police Woman* and *The Blues Brothers,* just to name a few.

A huge thanks goes out to Karen Rooney, the daughter of Tom Sweet, for the countless emails and corrections.

Also, thanks for all the support, Jody Sweet, Sherry Ogden Brooks, and Junior (Mo) Ogden.

Contents

INTRODUCTION

There was a point about five years ago when I figured I'd better start capturing some of these crazy stories I had. Growing up in the shadow of the motion picture industry, surrounded by rowdy stuntmen always doing something dangerous or crazy, seemed a no-brainer for an entertaining book; not to mention some of the unorthodox experiences I've had myself. So, yes, I grew up in the shadow of a giant, who doubled John Wayne and other notables, and did some wildly crazy stuff, but life had also flung an assortment of hard-to-believe stories at me as well. Like drawing a deadly mob figure undercover for a TV network and navigating the roaring rapids of the Kern River without a life jacket. I guess when you're the son of a stuntman, you tend to do some pretty risky stuff. But living life without a net seemed to be pretty normal growing up and it must have just rubbed off.

If I travel back into those first memories, I trigger those vague recollections of what it was like early on with my dad. Being little back then, I remember his size. He was, literally, like a giant compared to me. Not one that you would fear necessarily, although he would later become famous for doing just that when he portrayed Jason Voorhees in *Friday the 13th The Final Chapter*. But he knew how to be silly and that quality made him very accessible, especially to a kid. I liked what Mike Meyers said about his dad: *Being serious was something he had to do occasionally, before he could get back to being silly again.* Now, it may not have been my dad's constant state of mind, but it was one of his attributes that I remember and treasure most.

There were days when he would say, *"Come on, let's weld something together in the garage, Mikey."* And by the end of the day we had designed a metal sculpture, welded together from old motorcycle parts, of a motorcycle rider mid-crash. Our garage was a big kid's playground. We had mini bikes, go-carts, motorcycles, motorcycles with sidecars, model airplanes and an occasional rocket. There was always something fun or dangerous to do. My poor mother probably had no fingernails left from biting them off for fear we'd kill ourselves. But, my brother Ted and I were taught to respect those toys and learned the right way to use them. Even though once when Ted was driving the go-cart, the gas pedal stuck and plowed right into my dad, cutting him off at the ankles and sending him flying into the flowerbed. Ahhh, good times.

However, there was a line that was drawn. We couldn't be stuntmen. He wouldn't even tolerate the conversation. It was out of the question. Something my brother and I resented, vehemently, at first. So, we went our different directions and left the dream of becoming like dad. It wasn't until years later, after learning that my buddy, Reid Rondell, who *had* followed in his dad's footsteps, had been killed doing a stunt. My dad's words now had a new and different ring to them.

I remember once when I was about seven or eight, my dad suggested we take the motorcycle and sidecar out for a ride. Back then we lived in Arleta, California. Excitedly, I got in the sidecar and my dad and I took off on our adventure. I didn't know where we were going, nor did I care. I was with my dad on an adventure and I could only imagine where we might wind up.

There was a stuntman friend of my dad's, named Lennie Gear, who lived in Topanga Canyon. If you remember Hitchcock's *The Birds*, Lennie was the guy who ran into the glass phone booth with blood all over his face, screaming while the birds were attacking from every which direction.

It seemed like we drove forever to get there. Lennie lived right by the creek in the canyon amongst the tall, shady trees. Built into these trees, were platforms you could climb up onto and he had a large air mattress on the ground below. Many stunt guys used to go out to Lennie's place and practice their high falls. Lennie had trained dogs and cats, too. He'd rent them out to be in the movies. These animals knew lots of cues and could also do tricks. Lennie would give a cue and his cat would ride on the dog's back. It was an amazing place that I'll never forget. I wanted so much to be a part of it, but couldn't.

However, my brother Ted and another stuntman's son, Junior, did secretly go out to Lennie's, a dozen or so times. Lennie was teaching them how to do fights and high falls. That is, until my dad got wind of it and put the kibosh on the whole thing.

The main point of this book is to remember one thing: You can watch the game of life from the grandstands or you can get down on the field and get dirty. If you never get in the game and throw the dice, you never have a shot at winning. Playing it safe was never part of our family's mindset. I guess that's why I have a bunch of crazy, dysfunctional stories to tell.

So, I hope you'll enjoy this book of stories. And remember, this stuff actually happened. Yes, the years have probably given way to a bit of embellishment here and there, but none-the-less, they're true. Some are stories that are part of American pop culture—what happened behind-the-scenes. Some are stories that shaped our lives and will live on to be handed down to our children and our children's children.

My dad always told to me to write about interesting people doing interesting things. So, I've taken his advice. After all, how many of us can say, "We grew up in the shadows of giants"?

Chapter 1
A Rocky Start

As soon as I could walk, I grabbed a bottle of Pine Sol and downed it—toddler with a death wish? Maybe. Maybe, somehow I knew I had been born into a not-so-normal family and wanted to nip it in the bud. But, they pumped my stomach and stuck me in a crib to keep me safe from myself. That didn't work, either. I shook it so hard all the screws fell out. So, they got me a bed and figured, if he falls out on his head, that's his problem. I wasn't even getting paid and I was the world's first stunt baby.

My mom, Rosemary, was a fashion illustrator. She worked for Gimbels Department stores, Fredrick's of Hollywood, and many others. She painted beautiful, sexy watercolors of women. And, not only was she an amazing artist, but she was a beauty queen as well; voted Mrs. Oklahoma City in the Oklahoma beauty pageant. I remember seeing an old, yellowed newspaper clipping at some point, with the write-up and a photograph of her with the sash across her chest. I'd give anything to have that clipping still. But the years have taken so much away—including her.

But, before my parents were married and my brother and I came along, my dad, Alex, (nicknamed Ted) was a

Marine in World War II. He returned home to Oklahoma with a Purple Heart from being wounded and a battlefield commission as a Lieutenant before getting involved in some nefarious jobs.

US Marines Alex Bayouth, Jr. (middle) and his two PFC buddies

He sold used cars for a spell before he and his Marine buddies concocted a wild scheme to borrow Coca Cola's recipe and sell the popular beverage—illegally. You could say my dad was a kind of wise guy back then—

carried a gun and everything. Dad hung out at this place called Koche's Dance Hall every night where he met up with a couple of his war buddies. There was Tappy Simon, who was a gunner on a B-17 back from Europe and Johnny (The Greek) Gallipolis who was a second Lieutenant in the Navy.

So the story goes, that they were at the local drug store one day and had ordered a sandwich and a Coke. Well, they didn't have any Coke because sugar was rationed back then by the Office of Price Administration (OPA). This, in turn, caused the soft drink to become scarce. And that got my dad thinking. He figured he'd call the OPA and tell them, that as an ex-marine, he wanted to make a finished 5-cent drink and see if he could use his GI Bill to get some sugar. He was told by the OPA to present his discharge papers and, low and behold, they agreed to give him ten thousand pounds of sugar per month!

On the back of the syrup bottle that Coke sells, there is the recipe for how to make it. So, they went to Coca Cola and purchased fifty empty gallon bottles and got a 150-gallon round, aluminum drum, that you'd water cattle with, added the sugar and made their own Coca Cola syrup. They figured it cost them about 30-cents a gallon to make it. They called the drink AAA Cola and took it around to stores to sell. They sold it for $3.95 a gallon and sold out in two days!

After Tappy and Johnny used their G.I. bills as well, they were pulling down thirty thousand pounds of sugar a month. For the amount of money they were making, you'd think they were dealing the other kind of coke. My dad bought a brand new Oldsmobile convertible and moved into the Adolphus Hotel in Oklahoma City. He was Breaking Bad and living in fat city.

About five months later, a bootlegger, who ran a local still, got wind of their operation and approached Johnny Gallipolis to sell him four or five hundred pounds of their sugar. A deal was struck and their sugar operation began to expand.

Two weeks later, the Federal Marshall raided the bootlegger's still and confiscated the entire outfit, including the sugar bags. The sugar bags carried the OPA logo and a serial number that were printed on each one of them, which left a sweet, white trail right back to AAA Cola. The next day, all three of them were arrested.

A week later, an article came out in the local newspaper about the arrest, referring to my dad as "The Sugar Daddy of Oklahoma City." The papers detailed how they were selling Coca Cola syrup. A few days after that, they were all sued for a million dollars by the Coke corporation. My dad's Oklahoma Coke cartel had been brought to its knees.

Shortly after that, they made bricks of soap from leftover restaurant fat and sold it to car washes. But their chemistry was a tad off because they put too much lye in it. This excess amount of lye caused an unforeseen outcome at the carwash. It stripped the paint off the cars!

So, the police escorted Johnny (The Greek) Gallipolis out of town, telling him he had to go back to Chicago. Tappy Simon went to work for the United States Post Office delivering mail, and my dad married my mom.

Chapter 2
California Or Bust!

We moved to Hollywood, more specifically, The San Fernando Valley, leaving the headlines and the million dollar lawsuits behind. Before my dad met John Wayne he started out swimming with sharks for Andy Griffith.

Dad was starting out doing some work as an extra in the movie business. It was on his first job working in an Andy Griffith film called *Onion Head*, that he swam with sharks in the ocean. This was truly stunt work, rather than the typically benign work as an extra.

This work lead to a referral from Griffith to play an escaped convict on *The Andy Griffith Show*. He played the character of Avery Noonan and actually had some dialogue, to boot! He was moving fast but this was only the calm before the storm …

Ted White on the set of "The Andy Griffith Show"
playing escaped convict, Avery Noonan

Chapter 3
The Duke Days

My dad met John Wayne briefly when he was hired as a Marine Corp consultant on *The Sands of Iwo Jima.* Later, he would do a series of movies with the Hollywood icon that eventually ended in an almost fist fight during the filming of *Hatari.* But I'll get to that in a minute.

My dad stands six foot four, roughly the size of John Wayne, so he became Wayne's stunt double working on other Duke films including *Rio Bravo*, *Horse Soldiers*, *The Alamo* and *Hatari.*

Dad spent six months in Africa during the filming of *Hatari.* He captured wild gazelles, zebras, wildebeest and many other untamed animals—all while performing his other obligations of doing stunts for several of the actors, including the Duke, himself.

In one scene of the film, the script called for the Indian character to be gored by a rhino while driving a jeep. Carey Loftin was the stunt driver on the show but my dad insisted Carey sit this one out. They were the only two stuntmen on the film. If both of them got injured or killed, who would do the remaining stunts? So my dad rode as a passenger while a hunting professional, known as the white hunters, drove the jeep.

Ted White riding passenger doing a dangerous
stunt with a wild rhino in "Hatari"

Now, you might ask how one goes about getting a shot like this since there is no such thing as a "tame" rhino. Basically, they had to antagonize one in its natural habitat. No kidding. I just can't imagine them saying, "Yeah, it can be done. We'll just make the rhino real mad." So, just how exactly does this work, anyway? And how do you get the rhino mad enough to get its horn a few inches from the stuntman's leg to get the shot and not actually gore him? Is there a controlled degree of pissed-offness you can provoke in a rhino? I don't know about you, but if I was my dad, I'd sure want to know. I haven't checked, but I don't think there's a book called "How To Piss Off A Rhino."

So the rhino would give chase and my dad would cat and mouse with the wild rhino with the jeep until the rhino literally attacked it. Well, it worked. In fact, on the first take, the rhino flipped the jeep over with my dad in it. That alone could have gotten him killed. Just to give you an idea how powerful this animal is, its horn punctured the metal frame of the jeep and poked a hole in the gas tank. In a sequence of photographs from this scene I have framed in my home, it clearly shows gas streaming out of the jeep's tank from the rhino having gored it. Better that, than my dad's leg!

Finally, the rhino rammed the jeep without flipping it, and its horn came intimately close to my dad's leg. Dad instantly broke a blood squib, reacted in pain and they got the shot. I can imagine asking him at the end of his day, "So dad, how was your day at work?" Right?

Also, during the filming of *Hatari*, my dad became a local hero for saving a woman and her baby from Africa's most deadly animal.

The story goes like this. Dad was practicing his rope skills by roping a tree stump that was in the production compound with his lariat. Being good at roping was important for any stuntman on this film. When you are trying to catch wild animals, you'd better be a good roper, otherwise there will be many retakes and your credibility would slip. Now, let me set the stage for you here. A Cape buffalo is considered the most deadly and dangerous animal in Africa. Why, you might ask. Well, the Cape buffalo is a very robust species, notably tall in both size and ferocity. Many experts proclaim there is no animal more dangerous to man than a wounded African or Cape buffalo. They are prized by big game hunters due to their viciousness and are a member of the Big Five game animals along with elephants, lions, leopards, and rhinos. However, they are responsible for more human deaths than the others in this group of five. They are large animals with shoulders about 5 ½ feet off the ground. Males weigh up to 1750 pounds and females about 100 pounds less. What is strange is that both sexes have the fearsome horns. If a Cape buffalo is wounded, it will attack the hunter. This is done by circling around the hunter and stalking them.

Ted White and Russ Sauders on location in Africa
during the filming of "Hatari"

Ted White in Africa

The Cape buffalo waits for the right opportunity to charge the hunter and gore him with their horns. This animal will attack humans with the smallest provocation. With their ability to reach speeds of up to 35 mph, they can outrun lions and make difficult targets for humans. They are extremely difficult to kill instantly unless the shot hits their spine. The minimum safe caliber is a .375 Magnum from within 50 yards or less. This really increases the risk for the hunter. Get the picture? It's really a dangerous animal.

There were two Cape buffalo being guarded in a makeshift pen in the compound where the production company had set up camp. Many of these cages were made from the branches of trees fashioned together by the local natives and held many different animals for the production filming. The guard had gone to lunch and no one was watching the pen.

The production company's footprint was vast. This compound held many people working on the production; filming equipment, animals, transportation and housing. For all intents and purposes, it was like a temporary city.

A mother was pushing her baby in a stroller across the compound while my dad was practicing roping the stump. One of the Cape buffalo jumped out of its unguarded holding pen and charged the woman and her baby. You can imagine how terrifying this must have been.

John Wayne and Ted White on the set of
"Horse Soldiers"

Ted White on the set of "Rio Bravo" with John Wayne
and Dean Martin

My dad saw the animal and aptly roped it around the neck on the first toss. He ran to a nearby tree and dallied around it several times with the rope and tied it off. When the buffalo hit the end of the rope, he flipped upside down and hit the dirt hard but sprang back up like a cat. The animal now turned and trained his attack on my dad who quickly backed away until the animal hit the end of the rope again and went down.

My dad was an instant hero. The only problem was, it wasn't John Wayne. Yes, the Duke had an ego the size of Texas. It was the only thing bigger than his celebrity. Apparently, this little off-camera, real life stunt didn't sit well with the Duke, especially after a local Nairobi rag got wind of it and the story was printed in the paper.

At the end of the next day, after the article had made it to print, my dad entered the local cast and crew watering hole. The Duke was already there and had consumed a few too many. My dad sat down a few bar stools away and ordered a drink. The Duke looked down the bar and said, "That's a cheap goddamn way of gettin' your name in the paper." And then, under his breath added, "For two cents, I'd kick your ass." My dad reacted, instinctively grabbing a handful of change on the bar and throwing it in the Duke's direction saying, "That oughta cover it!" The two huge men went for each other. Fortunately, they were held apart by crew members.

It was a very tense moment that could have had vast repercussions on the entire production.

The next morning, Howard Hawks, the director, called my dad off to one side and asked, "Ted, did you have a problem with the Duke last night?" My dad told him what had transpired. Hawks then asked, "Would you have whipped him?" My dad replied, "So fast he wouldn't have even known what happened."

Hawks shared his concerns of how it might have put the whole production in jeopardy. My dad realized this was true and agreed to talk with Wayne.

When the Duke arrived on set, my dad walked up to him and the Duke said, "You got any more change?"

"No." my dad replied. "I should have never said a thing."

The Duke said, "You had every right to do what you did." They shook hands and that was the end of it.

I met John Wayne twice, years later—once, at *The Tonight Show Staring Johnny Carson*, where I worked at NBC and later at the Rose Parade when he was on a float. I ran into the street and shook his hand. I'm lucky I didn't get shot.

Chapter 4
Stuntman & The Tiger

When *Hatari* was over, Director Howard Hawks was saying his goodbyes to the cast and crew who were leaving the Serengeti for Nairobi and headed for different parts of the world. He handed my dad a mysterious white envelope, and said, "Here Ted, this is for you." Several days prior, Hawks had asked my Dad if he had enjoyed the experience and if he had gotten to hunt all the animals he wanted to.

Now you have to consider, back in 1962, animal rights and that entire consciousness regarding the hunting and killing of animals had not yet come to pass. Suffice it to say, Hawks, Duke and my dad all had conquered the Big Five while in Africa, so it was very much a part of the experience, especially for "real men."

When asked this, my dad told Hawks that he had a wonderful time but told him some day he wanted to come back to India and get a tiger.

Ted White in Kabar, India on a killer tiger hunt

Now it was time to leave on the airplane and my dad was holding this mysterious white envelope from Hawks. My dad opened it and there was the paperwork for a ten-day tiger hunt in India. My dad changed his flight that day to New Delhi, India instead of Rome.

After reaching New Delhi, he met two white hunters who worked for the government. The three of them travelled inland about three hundred miles to a very old village of six or seven hundred people. No electricity, no running water, just huts. There he found out it wasn't just any tiger they would be hunting; it was an old tiger that had killed many young children and elders in the village.

They travelled four days into the interior with a tracking party. On the fifth day at about sundown, on a narrow path, one of the white hunters who was in front of my dad, stopped. He held up his hand, listened and circled his index finger. My dad had no idea what this meant until the hunter behind him tapped him on the shoulder and whispered, "Look up." There was a bluff about ten feet high above them shrouded in foliage—they couldn't see anything but the greenery. They continued to move closer as the foliage cleared. There it was, crouched, ready to spring; the enormous creature that had be wreaking havoc on that small village. My dad positioned his rifle, as the man-eater rose up to pounce. He squeezed the trigger and with one shot, killed it, instantly.

He felt good about the hunt and ending the fear this animal had created but did not take part in the celebratory Indian tradition of eating the animal that had plagued their village. The government later sent him the tiger-skin rug with the entire head and teeth in a fierce, snarling grimace.

We grew up with this incredibly scary and morbid thing in our house and my dad still owns it to this day.

It was no big deal when I was a little kid but thinking back on it now, it's really strange how we lived with this thing on the floor in our house. There were many occasions when this tiger-skin rug became the perfect thing to scare somebody with. All you had to do was get underneath it late at night and lay in wait. The victims of this prank would meet it with blood-curdling screams and a mad dash to the bathroom.

Chapter 5
Cat Ballou

My Dad's cameo in *Cat Ballou* is probably one of my favorites—and he's had his share of other cameos, too; like the opening scene in *Romancing the Stone*; his menacing performance in *Against All Odds;* and the red-neck deer hunter in *Starman*. But *Cat Ballou* was one of my dad's favorite comedies.

He and Lee Marvin hung out a lot together and, both Marines—they had that war buddy bond. They did *Ship of Fools* and several other movies and TV shows together. Lee, like so many other actors, loved to hang around with stuntmen and hear their stories. My dad's cameo in the film comes when Jane Fonda is waiting in town for the arrival of her hired gunslinger to avenge her father's death. The stagecoach pulls up and she excitedly waits for this hired killer to emerge. My dad, dressed from hat to boot in black, and looking like a fierce gunslinger, emerges from the stage coach and Fonda's character assumes he is her gun-for-hire. Wowed by his foreboding presence, she is quickly disappointed as his wife and five small children rush into his arms. Clearly, this family man was not the gunman she was waiting for.

Then, in a drunken pile of dust and crumpled clothing, the real, and less ominous gunslinger, played by Lee Marvin, stumbles out from the baggage hold.

I was fortunate to have met Lee Marvin as well. In my career at NBC, they began sending me out on courtroom illustration assignments. One of these cases turned out to be Lee Marvin's palimony trial. I was the artist for thirteen weeks on the *Marvin vs. Marvin* trial and what a spectacle it was. During one recess, I introduced myself to Lee as Ted White's son. From that point on Lee took me under his wing because my dad and he were so tight.

One recess he was talking to me and asked, "You know what the secret to all this legal stuff is, kid?" I responded with, "No. What, Lee?"

"Who has the best script," he answered. Well, I laughed out loud and later was asked by an *LA Times* reporter what we had talked about. After I relayed the comment, it wound up being printed in the *LA Times* the next morning, unquoted, thank God. The judge reprimanded the *Times* reporter for it as I sunk down in my chair hoping Lee did not remember our conversation. It almost caused a mistrial.

Cat Ballou went on to be nominated for five Academy Awards with Lee Marvin winning the Oscar for Best Actor.

Michael Bayouth

Chapter 6
Fire Ants!

The driveway in our backyard was covered in ants one day when my dad said, "What do we do with all these ants, Mikey?" Of course, there were many smart answers to this question, like Black Flag ant killer, soapy water or just plain ol' insecticide. But to ask a seven-year-old kid this kind of a question, I only had one answer: "Burn 'em, Dad!"

So, my dad, being not of sound mind nor thought, listened to me and got the gasoline. He dumped out several gallons covering the ants and told me to back up. He tossed a lit match on it and a giant, black mushroom cloud rose high into the air. It was the coolest thing that I had ever seen and, from the look on my dad's face, it was much bigger than he expected.

The fire department was stationed just a block away and the next thing we knew a several alarm fire was sounded and two large fire trucks were dispatched to our house with a hook and ladder. Firemen streamed into our backyard, expecting a large-scale inferno. My dad did some quick back-pedaling.

"My kid just wanted me to burn some ants, was all. Why don't you guys come inside and I'll tell you about some of the movies I've done?"

Throughout the years, I've watched my dad play the "Hollywood stuntman card" and sidestep trouble. He was good at it and that's exactly what he did this time, too.

He took all the firemen inside, made them drinks and told them stories of movies he'd done and his tales of working with giant celebrities. They all left about an hour later, laughing and stumbling to their fire engines—another great moment in backyard politics.

Chapter 7
The Tree House Mystery

Before leaving for Africa, my dad built my brother Ted and me an awesome treehouse in the backyard. This was a very special treehouse. It had a ladder leading up to it with a secret way to get in; a trap door in the floor that was controlled with a rope by whoever was inside. This was HQ central for my brother and me. And on hot summer nights, we'd sleep up there. It was very much a part of our childhood magic.

One humid, summer evening, my brother and I decided to take our sleeping bags, some popcorn, and a couple of cokes to go sleep in the treehouse. We got inside and then pulled the rope up through the hole in the floor and were securely hunkered down for the night.

Later that night, we heard someone, ever so slowly, ascending the steps of the ladder. We froze in terror. By the time the footsteps reached the top we were beside ourselves in fear. Whoever it was, just stayed there, right outside the door, not moving, not even breathing. We never even heard the sound of any descending footsteps. Nothing. We just sat there frozen, like a couple of jerks till the sun came up.

Now, when you're a kid and this happens, the pictures and thoughts that run through your head are not pretty. In fact, they become downright horrific.

So, for the rest of the summer my brother and me decided to move our headquarters back into the safety of our house. After much questioning, my mom swore she hadn't come out to check on us and with my dad out of town, it has remained an unsolved mystery to this day.

Chapter 8
Pony Express!

My brother and I occasionally got too creative trying to figure out what to do with our spare time. Let's see, dad's gone on location, there are ponies in the backyard and we have a red wagon. Let's make a pony express! Right? Wrong.

My dad had built an entire wooden barn and stables in our backyard in Woodland Hills. It was a classic, rust-red barn for keeping horses. Horses were a big part of our lives growing up. And, back in those days, stuntmen needed horses for doing stunts in Westerns, which were still very much a part of movie pop culture. A horse you could count on for a safe saddle fall or a horse fall was as important as a racecar was to a driver. They had to be ridden and kept trained for whenever that call might come in from the studios. For a short while, we even kept the horse in our backyard from the film *Cat Ballou* that was trained to sit down on cue.

My brother Ted and I each had our own horse. My brother's horse was a mare named Flip but Ted called her Flipper. My horse was a grey-spotted Appaloosa named Beaver. (Believe me, I didn't name her.) If people didn't know us, they'd think we owned a dolphin and a rodent.

Christmas was just around the corner, so my dad and his stuntman friend, Morry Ogden, bought these twelve Shetland Ponies at auction. Their plan was to sell them off to people for holiday gifts to their kids. But after they brought them back to our stables, they realized they were anything but tame. Their tails and manes were tangled and full of heckle-burrs. They weren't used to human beings or even being in captivity, for that matter. They would run full bore, head-on into the fences without it even fazing them. Not the smartest animals in the corral, that's for sure.

It finally dawned on my dad and Morry that, who in their right mind would ever buy one of these dirty dozen for their kids? It would be like signing the kid's death warrant. My brother Ted and his friend Junior, tried to ride one and nearly got themselves killed.

So, the story goes like this: My dad was on location working on a film so Ted, Junior and I got it in our heads to create a pony express with one of these wild Shetland ponies. There was a riding area in front of our barn and stable which was the perfect place to attempt this nutty idea. We managed to get close enough to hook one of the ponies up with some lariat rope to our red metal wagon that was lying around in the backyard. This was going to be a blast, we thought. We'll take turns in the wagon getting pulled around the riding area like a real pony express. Well, it seemed like a good idea at the time, anyway.

We got it all set up. Ted got in the wagon and we let go of the pony. It immediately spooked and took off running, flipping the wagon over and sending Ted face down into the dirt. The pony, dragging a clanging wagon behind it, became terrified and began running wild in circles. We gave chase but the pony was way too fast.

As it ran amuck in larger circles, the wagon swung wide behind it. Then, the wagon wrapped itself around one of the four support posts that held up the overhanging barn roof and tore the post out of its foundation like a toothpick. This unbridled mayhem continued as we chased the out-of-control pony, dragging the overturned wagon behind it. On the next lap, the wagon tore out yet another post.

"Oh no!" we thought. The barn roof was beginning to collapse! We tried to stop it but it was almost impossible. Neighbors looked on in shock. The better idea was to have probably sold tickets.

We finally managed to get a hold of the wild pony and put it back in its stall.

When my dad came home and saw the damage, he asked my mother, "What the hell happened to my barn?" She responded by saying, "Oh, the kids were playing pony express with the wagon." Needless to say, we both were grounded. We had to help fix the barn, and the ponies, well, they went back to the auction house.

How exciting it was. A small-scale, action sequence in our very own backyard! It, literally, brought the barn down.

Chapter 9
Glow For It!

This is one of those brief experiences that have to be highlighted in bright yellow. I mean really bright yellow.

My Mom wanted a fresh coat of paint on the house, so she set my dad to task. Thinking smart, my dad purchased the paint at a garage sale and saved a bundle of money—such a smart shopper. It was cadmium yellow, to which my mom smiled and approved. So, my dad started Saturday morning and worked all weekend getting the job expertly done.

At the end of the weekend, to celebrate the results of all his hard work, he took us all out for dinner. When we returned to the house the sun had gone down and it was dark out—except for something that was glowing at the end of our street—our HOUSE! The paint my Dad had purchased from the garage sale was NOT regular paint. This bright yellow paint was a highly toxic, lead chromate reflective paint used to paint yellow lines on roads! Our house glowed like it was on fire. The neighbors were all standing around looking at the spectacle as if they were waiting for Jesus to appear from the front door. Clark Grizwold would have been proud. My Dad had to repaint the entire house. Lesson learned. Moving on.

Michael Bayouth

Chapter 10
It's All In The Wrist

The longest recorded laugh in TV history was when Ed Ames appeared on *The Tonight Show Starring Johnny Carson* to demonstrate how to throw a tomahawk. Three guesses who taught him how to throw it?

At that time, dad was the longest running, contracted stuntman in Hollywood. He was the stunt coordinator and doubled for Fess Parker in the *Daniel Boone* TV series from 1964 to 1970. I'll never forget when I turned 14; my Dad took me to the set with him. Fess made my birthday very special, sending the prop man out to buy me a dragster model. I loved it. As if that wasn't enough, at the end of the day Fess walked over to me and said, "Son, I'd like you to have something very special." He pulled his bowie knife from his knee-high moccasin and handed it to me. I was completely blown away. I said, "But don't you need it?" He assured me that he'd have another one made by the prop department and that I should have his for my real birthday present. I still have it. Now that Fess has passed away, I treasure it like a relic from King Tut's tomb.

Later on, Ed Ames came on the show to play the Native American, Mingo. Being the stunt coordinator for the show, my dad was responsible to teach Ed how to throw a tomahawk and to use a bullwhip. He also taught him to use a bow and arrow and occasionally he had to double for him when stunts were required. This required my dad to look just like Mingo.

I remember one time my dad came home in full Mohawk Indian regalia. He donned war paint, a Mohawk hairpiece that covered a bald cap and he carried a tomahawk. He knocked at the front door and I answered it. "Holy crap!" I gasped. My dad put his finger to his lips and whispered one question to me, "Where's your mother?" Smiling, I pointed to the bathroom, where I knew she was fixing herself up. He tippy-toed in and raised the tomahawk over his head as he stealthy made his way back to the bathroom. I had to see this for myself, so I quietly followed behind.

He opened the door and let out an Indian war cry that would have made Cochise proud. My mom let out a scream that could have woken the dead. She chased my dad out of the bathroom with her hairbrush. I think that was the only time in history that a hairbrush was more deadly than a tomahawk.

Ted White, Darby Hinton and Ed Ames on location
during the filming of the "Daniel Boone" TV series

Which leads me to Ed Ames' tomahawk story. For those of you unfamiliar with Ed's visit to *The Tonight Show Starring Johnny Carson,* the story goes like this: Ed was enjoying his stint on the *Daniel Boone* show when he was invited on *The Tonight Show.* On Carson, he was asked to demonstrate his prowess of how to throw a tomahawk as he did in the TV show.

Carson had a wooden, life-size cutout of a man made for the purpose of this demonstration on stage. Ed got in position, standing a good twenty feet away from the target. He seemed so professional and was not joking around in the least. This was serious business. A hush fell over the crowd. When you think about it, it actually was kind of dangerous. If it didn't go right, it could have glanced off the target and into the audience and possibly killed someone.

Ed said, rocking back and forth on his left heel, "It's all in the wrist, Johnny. It all in the wrist." He took a few practice swings before he threw it. He then focused his concentration as everyone in the live audience held their breath. Ed threw the tomahawk. It made several revolutions and stuck firmly into the wooden cutout of the man—right in the crotch! The tomahawk pointed straight up like an erection. The crowd instantly became unglued with laughter.

Ed immediately ran to retrieve the tomahawk from the target sporting the woody, but Johnny stopped him in his tracks and pulled him away. Carson recognized this comedic, gold moment and seized it like the pro he was. A precious prize, a gift no one could have even hoped for, or planned on; a real showstopper. In fact, it was the longest recorded laugh in the history of *The Tonight Show.*

Johnny, nonchalantly began to sharpen the two additional tomahawks he held in his hands as the audience roared on and on. If it were in color you would have seen Ed Ames turn a crimson red, I'm sure. History was made that night and I give full credit to the man who taught Ed Ames the proper way to throw that tomahawk- —my dad!

Michael Bayouth

Chapter 11
Grizzly Bear Scare

One of the greatest practical jokes of all time had to have been the running one between my dad and Fess Parker. Some of this may be considered *blue humor.* However, since we are talking about two adult, grown men in show business, it only adds to the dysfunctional entertainment of it all.

During my dad's time on the *Daniel Boone* show, Fess invited my dad to join him on an episode of *The American Sportsman* featuring Fred Bear. Fess was the guest celebrity on the show that week and my dad was to come along as his personal bodyguard. The episode was shot in British Columbia and centered on hunting for grizzly bear.

Now, you have to understand, Fess and my dad, at this point in time, had played many a practical joke on one another. On the set, they used to shoot Polaroid pictures of each other's butts to see who had the bigger of the two. They would go so far as to cut out the butt from the picture if it was too incriminating.

We pick up the action in British Columbia on *The American Sportsman.* This was grizzly bear country and they were advised to be vigilant. Fess was a bit nervous even though he had his bodyguard present. My dad brought his camera and hoped to get some good photos while there. They were camped out in the woods and it was getting dark.

Dinner detail had just finished and any leftover food was being carefully wrapped up and locked away. A small campfire was started and the crew began battening down the hatches for the night.

My dad noticed Fess get up and say, "Well, nature calls," and head off into the woods. Taking care of your business in the woods amounts to keeping a flattened roll of toilet paper in your shorts and finding a good secluded spot.

After Fess left, a devious thought went through my dad's head. He grabbed his camera and took off. Quiet as a mouse, dad stalked Fess to his secluded spot. My dad parked himself behind some thick foliage so as not to be seen. He managed to get the lens of his camera through a spot where he could get a clear picture. Fess dropped trou. My dad began making a low growl like a grizzly bear. Fess' eyes bulged white with terror. This can't be happening, he thought! I'm supposed to get the grizzly bear, not the other way around. Then, a louder growl came from the bush nearby and Fess switched into full panic mode. His first impulse was, of course, to run. But with his pants around his ankles, this was impossible. My dad began to really lay it on thick now, "Rahhhhhhh-AHHHHHH!"

At this, Fess fell backwards into his own mess. Picture time! The motor drive on my dad's Nikon rattled off 10 shots per second but couldn't be heard over my dad roaring so loud. It was a bonanza of bad photos in beautiful Kodachrome color. The most compromising shots you could ever imagine and, yet, Fess didn't even realize my dad was there.

Fess made it back to camp, panting. He was white as a sheet. "A grizzly almost got me," he said as he tried to catch his breath. My dad had already made it back to camp with his feet up resting on a rock and camera stowed safely away. My dad asked with concern, "Really? Are you okay?" Fess immediately had to go down to the stream and wash up as he carried a hefty stench with him. It was now confirmed to the members of the camp that a bear really could scare the shit out of you!

During the whole trip, Fess never found out that my dad had done this. The show wrapped when Fess eventually got his bear and they returned home.

It wasn't until they got back to the *Daniel Boone* show that Fess discovered what my dad had done. Every time Fess would walk into his dressing room you could hear him yell out in horror as he discovered another 11 x 14 inch glossy, color print of the uncompromising series my dad had secretly photographed. Although it seemed like my dad had the upper hand with this practical joke, Fess took it all in stride and I'm sure Fess got his payback too.

Ted White and Fess Parker on location during
the filiming of "Daniel Boone"

Chapter 12

Mom on Fire!

My mom caught on fire in the kitchen one morning cooking breakfast for my brother and me. My dad saved her as if it was all in a day's work. This is one of my faves because my brother and I had a front row seat. These stories within these chapters are mostly about things that were very dysfunctional, dumb or dangerous and so my mother gets glossed over a bit because she was none of these things in my life. She had to do something pretty extraordinary to take the spotlight away from us— like catch on FIRE! This did grab our attention even though it was unintentional. But before I get to the meat of this story, I want to share some details about my mom.

By the time I was five or six, I realized what a talented artist my mom was. I would watch her doodle while she was on the phone. They were masterpieces; sexy, full-figured women with full lips and long eyelashes. She'd throw them away after a long call with one of her girlfriends and then I'd go fish them out of the trash and marvel at them. I became very interested in this elusive ability of hers so I started asking questions—a lot of them. Sometimes when my parents would go out for dinner, I'd grab a coloring book and do the best I could to impress her. She'd return and I'd show her what I had done. Then came a lesson. It didn't matter how late it was. She always took time to help me improve what I had done and how to make it better. She'd blow me away with how good she was at even just coloring—bolding over the black lines that were already there with the crayon and then lightly, in the same direction, coloring in the interiors. This was amazing to me and fostered my interest even more!

Later on, she worked with me on drawing human anatomy. Gridding out the human head to properly show me where the eyes, nose and mouth went. Then there was drawing the female head in profile. She had it down. Four slightly curved lines floating on a white sheet of paper quickly became a sexy profile of a woman. Each of the lines represented the brow, nose, lips and the chin. From there it was just a matter of filling in the missing spaces but you could already see the face so vividly. She spent hours and hours with me sharing her secrets and I soaked them up like a sponge. To this day I owe all my artistic skills to her. It's hard to believe those coloring book and sketchpad lessons lead me along the path to a career as the artist I am today. Thanks mom!

So, back to the story about how my mom almost went up in smoke. One morning she was cooking breakfast for my brother and me. It was not unusual for the two of us to tear through a pound of bacon and a mountain of toast at any given breakfast. In fact, you could get a nasty fork stab if your timing was just a tad off which shows how fast and furious food would disappear off the platter. Mom cooked eggs, French toast and cowboy potatoes. Her breakfasts were the best!

She had just finished frying the bacon and removed the skillet but inadvertently left the flame on. When she reached across for the eggs on the back burner, her fluffy, white terry-cloth robe that she wore over her nightclothes, caught fire. Oblivious to the fact that she was on fire, she lowered her arm back to her side. Ted and I noticed the flames moving up her arm as my Dad walked into the kitchen. In an instant Mom's entire side and back were ablaze! Ted and I, who already had our mouths stuffed with greasy bacon, sat there in shock as my dad, who knew how to deal with fire gags, went directly to work. He grabbed her in his arms to douse the flames. She thought he was getting fresh with her, saying, "Oh Ted!" In one swift move, my Dad expertly grabbed the flaming robe, tore it off her shoulders and deposited it into a smoking pile of terry cloth on the kitchen floor. Mom still didn't know what was happening. Her hair had caught on fire in the back. My dad then bear hugged her. She disappeared into his huge frame and all we could see was smoke coming out of his arms against her muffled cries of resistance. She *still* didn't realize what was happening. Then, the fire was finally out. She was remarkably unscathed and only seemed to be upset about her robe.

"Why did you do that?" she asked my dad. We told her she was on fire. She took a moment, felt her smoldering hairdo and looked around the kitchen finally realizing how smoky it was. Then she noticed the shocked looks on our faces. At the motion picture studio, they both would have been paid handsomely for a fire gag like that.

"Oh," was all she said as she began cleaning up the mess. Now, *that* was a breakfast to remember.

Michael Bayouth

Chapter 13
All In My Head

I was about seven years old during the second season of the *Daniel Boone* show. They went to Kanab, Utah on location and I was lucky enough to get to go with my family. My brother Ted, Ed Ames' son Ron, and I all hung out together and had a blast. The company stayed at The Perry Lodge, made famous for all the western films that were done back in those days and all the celebrities who stayed there.

All us kids got to be in the show too, playing in the background in the Boonesborough Fort that still remains there to this day. We got to be in full wardrobe, having fun, marching around and playing in the background. But then something happened. Something big. My Dad told me they needed me to play a part in the show. I was so excited, I was beside myself.

I was to play the part of an Indian boy who was captured and Daniel Boone was going to set me free. I said, in astonishment, "Are you kidding!?" I was whisked away to the wardrobe department for the full on outfit and then to make-up and hair. I had long braids and darkened skin; and the whole nine yards. My dad was also dressed as my Indian captor. The set photographer began taking stills of us before we shot the scene. I was going to be a star!

Ron Ames (colonial hat), me (in suspenders)
other kid extras on the set of "Daniel Boone"

In the scene, my hands were tied together while I was led down a mountainside as a captive by my Native American dressed dad and fellow stuntman, Charlie Horvath, who was also playing an Indian. At the bottom of the mountain, they were to lead me under a large oak tree where Daniel Boone (Fess Parker) was to jump down from the tree and save me. That was the big scene. As you can imagine, this was a really huge experience for me and I relished every minute of it.

We started the scene at the top of the hill. The two men had me captive as we walked down the trail to the large oak tree. Fess jumped out of the tree and onto the two of them. He punched them out, then took out his bowie knife (which is now mine) and cut my leather ties. I then ran off into the proverbial sunset. It was as sweet as Hollywood gets for a seven-year-old kid and I was on cloud nine for months afterward, as you can imagine.

After we returned home, my butt was parked in front of that TV set every Sunday evening looking for my scene to air. The whole season went by. Nothing. I was crushed. My dad didn't have an explanation. I had somehow vanished from the *Daniel Boone* show. I showed so much promise, too. That could have been the beginnings of a really good reel.

Cut to 45 years later. My family and I were getting ready to go to my dad's house for Christmas dinner. I kept thinking about the lost footage. Then it hit me. Could it be that they never filmed it? No! No way. That would have been a lot to go through just to make a great experience for a kid and never even film it. But then I thought about it.

I'd have done the same for my kids in a heartbeat if I had the chance, crew or no crew, camera or no camera.

I sat back on the couch, relaxed my mind and closed my eyes and regressed back in time—back 45 years to Kanab, Utah. There I was. I was back on that mountain again—with my dad and Charlie Horvath. I stopped and looked around. There was no camera and no crew! It was all acted out but never filmed! It was all in my mind!

That night at Christmas dinner, I asked my dad to tell me the truth. He said, "No, Michael, it was never filmed but you thought it was and I didn't have the heart to tell you the truth."

Looking back, it was better than anyone could ever imagine. My dad gave me that memory better than any camera ever could.

Michael Bayouth and Ted White on the set
of the "Daniel Boone" TV Series

Chapter 14
Flips, Fights & Frights

FLIPS

Dar Robinson became one of Hollywood's greatest stuntmen. How he got into the business exactly, I'm not so sure. All I do know is this; when I was about eight-years-old, my mom thought it might be good a good idea to give bible study lessons to my brother and me. So, out of seemingly nowhere, Dar Robinson showed up on our front porch with a bible in his hand and a smile on his face. All my brother and I knew was that this young, handsome fellow, for some reason, wanted to teach us the word of God and was so earnest about doing just that. I don't remember much about those bible study lessons except that my brother and I always looked forward to them being over because Dar would do a back flip for us on our front lawn. We were amazed at his athletic ability. A few years later, after he quickly became a huge name in the stunt industry, we realized he only wanted to get in with my dad for advice on how to break into the business.

Soon he became the number one high fall guy in the business and kept on breaking his own records. When I worked at NBC TV in the graphic arts department, I heard he was to be a guest on *The Tonight Show Starring Johnny Carson.* It was around 1979 and I paid him a visit in the green room before he went on. He remembered me and we had a nice chat about his high fall history. I asked him, "So Dar, how high do you plan on going?" He answered, practically instantaneously, "Until I miss."

The most incredible stunt he ever did, in my opinion, was when he jumped out of an airplane without a parachute. The plane went into a dive. During his free fall, he managed to maneuver himself over next to the plane again and crawl back in. The plane would then level out and come back in for a landing. Amazing.

Dar Robinson's stunts were always well planned, and he never broke a bone in his 19-year Hollywood career. On November 21, 1986, on the set of the film *Million Dollar Mystery*, in a routine high speed motorcycle run on a mountain road, he hit some loose gravel and went straight off a cliff to his death. Two years later, in 1988, a documentary on his life was made entitled *The Ultimate Stuntman: A Tribute to Dar Robinson.*

The last three films in which Robinson worked — *Cyclone, Lethal Weapon,* and *Million Dollar Mystery*—are all dedicated to his memory. Richard Donner's dedication in the closing credits of *Lethal Weapon* reads "*This picture is dedicated to the memory of Dar Robinson / one of the motion picture industry's greatest stuntmen.*"

FIGHTS

Part of the colorful background of my upbringing was my dad getting into fistfights, occasionally. As far as my understanding goes from the ones I witnessed, they all seemed to be the fault of the other guy.

Once, shortly after my dad had bought a new home up in the hills, he decided to have some landscaping done. I guess rumor had gotten around among the workers that he was a stuntman. We just had new carpet put in and one of the workers, who had muddy shoes on, asked to use our bathroom. My dad said, "Just wipe your feet before you go in." The guy somehow took offense to this remark and said, "Hey, I won't even go in your fuckin' house." To which my dad replied, "You don't need to go wearing your feelings on your sleeve, I just asked you to wipe your feet, pal." The worker then added, "Oh, big, tough Hollywood stuntman." My dad then warned, "You'd better button up your lip before I knock you through that window, buddy." Well, the guy said something else but his words were clipped off by my dad's fist. *Pow!* The guy went flying backwards off the front porch. This was the amazing part: while he was flying backwards through the air, my dad landed two more solid punches before he hit the ground!

The guy got to his feet, scrambled up the hill and ran to his car. As he drove by, safely in his car, he yelled obscenities at my dad. I remembered my dad referring to this incident as "yard work." Ha!

The last family dinner I remember us all going out for, was one I'll never forget. My mom, dad, brother and I were all in the car headed west on Ventura Boulevard in the San Fernando Valley. We were looking for a place to have dinner. Each place we passed that was a good possibility was quickly ruled out because my dad had had an altercation there.

"Hey, how 'bout Rococo?" My mom asked. My dad replied, "Naw, I knocked out the bartender there."

"Oh, okay," she said, "How about this Mexican place then?"

"No," my dad answered, "I took out a booth there in a fight. There's a place up here, I know." But as we approached, he would remember, "Damn, we can't go there either, I knocked some guy over the bar." Suffice it to say, by the time we found a place we could stop, we had travelled a great distance and we wound up eating at a place in Thousand Oaks.

FRIGHTS

I learned from my father that scaring someone could be really fun. Kids would avoid our house like the plague on Halloween because my dad was known in the neighborhood for his hijinks. And, for this reason, we always had a lot of candy leftover.

When I was a young man, I loved masks and prosthetics. In fact, I collected stuff like that. On a Saturday, I would think nothing of putting on a full Planet of the Apes outfit to take care of business. I'd do my grocery shopping and banking, all the while, dressed like the star ape, Cornelius. I had no fear of making a colossal fool of myself.

I remember once going to *Burt Wheeler's Magic Shop* on Hollywood Boulevard and purchasing a great looking scary mask that covered your whole head. As cool as it was, it still wasn't scary enough for me. I took it home and painted it. I added hair from one of my mom's wigs and made it much more gory. It had one bloody eye and the other eye was a cut out that you looked through. It was a true work of hideous art. I had it for years and got a ton of mileage out of it. But I think the best thing I ever used it for was this story I'm about to tell you.

Years later, when I was in my forties and a family man, I lived in Canoga Park, California. In the summer months, every single morning, I would find discarded ice cream wrappers all over my lawn. It was something I could depend on, like clockwork. I'd wake up, and there they were; three ice cream wrappers on the grass and I never witnessed anyone doing it. The trash just somehow appeared during the night and it was really bugging me.

It wasn't until my family and I returned home late from a long drive back from my brother-in-law's house down in Laguna. It was maybe two o'clock in the morning and as we were going inside with sleeping children, I noticed these three teenage girls walk by. Then, it hit me, these three girls had to be my elusive lawn litterers!

I guess they used to stay up late, then go to *7-Eleven* and get ice cream. The distance it took them to travel back from *7-Eleven* was just the right amount of time for them to get the ice cream out of the bag and discard the wrappers on my lawn.

But tonight, all this was about to change as I waited for them to come back with their frozen treats. Little did they know that in the darkened recesses of my living room, I laid-in-wait with the lights off looking through the one eyehole of my hideous mask as the bloody eye for its long-awaited revenge.

Over my clothes, I wore a classic trench coat that I used for my Humphrey Bogart impersonation at the Comedy Store. The full head mask was tucked into my trench coat and I pulled on some Frankenstein boots that I happened to have in the closet. I was poised and ready for the sweet payback that they so deserved. A good scare, I thought, would surely deter them from ever passing our way again. And besides, it was all in good, clean fun.

Here they came with ice cream in hand and off came the wrappers, drifting down and settling onto my grassy lawn in the early morning dew. As they passed, I slipped out like a trained ninja. I momentarily hid behind a hedge, then quietly moved up behind them and matched their gate. I didn't want to just jump out and scare them. I wanted much more.

At first they were oblivious to my presence behind them. So I started breathing very hard inside my mask, which finally caused one of them to turn around.

Being inside my mask was like being inside of a movie camera. It was like me witnessing something second person. I felt like I was watching a movie—a very scary movie. The girl's face filled with horror when she saw the mask. Not the kind of horror you see from an actress in a B horror film, but *real* horror. When she screamed, it was so loud I remembered it hurting my ears. And my ears were covered in thick rubber and wig hair. The other two girls turned and screamed as well. The three of them broke and ran. I was right on their heels. I growled and snarled just inches behind them. The sounds I made matched the horror of the mask I was wearing and somehow I knew these three girls were thinking this was their last moments on God's green earth.

Two of them broke off right, the other, left. I stopped under the streetlight in the intersection and made myself a huge, hulking figure, bobbing and breathing there under the amber streetlight. One of the girls turned back, now a hundred feet away and screamed again at the sight of me and finally disappeared around the corner.

I never found another ice cream wrapper on my lawn again.

~~~~~~~

Ranking among the classics of my all time scares, involved my dad's old girlfriend, Angie. This was after my parents were divorced. I was about fifteen and I lived with my dad in a new housing development up in the hilly regions of the San Fernando Valley.

Our house was on a steep street and Angie's best friend, Leslie, happened to live next door to us on the down side of the hill with her husband. There were no fences or landscaping yet in this community so you could see their roof from our backyard, which gives you an idea how steep the hill was.

My dad was on location somewhere doing a film and I was at home alone. Leslie's husband was also out of town on business and Angie and Leslie were together next door and home alone as well. You see where this is going?

Well, night had just fallen and I got a call from Angie who said she and Leslie heard some noises and were scared. I stepped outside and looked down the hill at the house and saw no one and told her everything looked fine. That's when I realized that opportunity was knocking on my door, or rather on their door.

I ran into the garage and got my dad's deep-sea fishing pole and a roll of masking tape as I formulated the master plan in my head. I tied a heavy, ten-ounce fishing weight on the line about six feet away from the hook. I wrapped a large wad of masking tape around the weight until it was about the size of a lemon—a nice soft, but heavy, package. Then, I sat the pole down and opened the reel to release the line.

Under the blanket of darkness, I stealthy descended the hill as quiet as a church mouse. With the weight and hook in tow, I snuck down into their backyard, which had no fence around it.

I found a patio chair and quietly placed it in front of a large sliding glass door. Fortunately for me, the curtain was closed so I couldn't be seen. I stepped on the chair and reached their roofline. I dug the hook deep into the wood shingle at the edge then pulled on the line, giving it a good tug, testing it. It wasn't going anywhere. Then I carefully got down, put the chair back and proceeded back up the hill to my backyard and the fishing pole. I picked up the pole and reeled up the slack. I had successfully hooked into their house down below. The line went all the way from the fishing pole to the hook in the shingle above their sliding glass door. And six feet up from the hook was the soft ten-ounce weight. The stage was set. I had the power of God in my hands and I knew it. By letting out some slack, I could pound on their slider with the ten-ounce weight, then pull it back up again taut and it wouldn't be seen. Brilliant, if I do say so, myself!

I let the weight swing down and it pounded on the glass slider a few good times, then I pulled the line back up taut again. Angie and Leslie peeked through their curtains to see who was pounding, but no one was there.

"Ring!" went my phone again and I answered it. This time with a yawn, pretending I had fallen asleep on the couch. They were frantic. "Oh my God, Michael! Someone's trying to get in! Help us!" Angie gasped. I told her I would go outside and look again. After a few minutes, and a pretend glance at Leslie's house, I told her I saw no one. I suggested they were just hearing things and that they should ignore it which seemed to satisfy them. I was so happy that I actually jumped up and down. I don't ever remember having so much fun by myself.

I waited about five minutes or so and grabbed the pole again. Boom! Boom! Boom! I could almost hear the screams from below. It was sweet bliss.

Now, I know what you might be saying. Geez, that wasn't very nice. Or how could you be so cruel? It was fun. Yeah, I know, something could have gone wrong. But it didn't and I'm sure it spiced up their evening a lot. I know they weren't bored, that's for sure.

An hour or so later, I slipped back down the hill and undid the hook, putting all the incriminating evidence back in the garage. When my dad came back home, I told him what I had done. I don't think I ever saw him so proud of me.

Michael Bayouth

Chapter 15
Real Dumb Fun

Sometimes kids do real dumb stuff, like running with scissors, going swimming immediately after they eat, or shooting five miles of rapids without a lifejacket. Ya think?

When my buddy Jeff Mogalian and I were sixteen, we decided to get out of Dodge and go do some fishing and camping up at the Kern River. The heat of the summer was driving most people out of the Valley and we felt no different. So we packed up our ice chest, some beer, a couple of steaks; grabbed our sleeping bags, camping stuff and were off.

By the time we got into the area of the Kern, we started seeing signs. Signs that were very clear about the dangers involved with going in the waters of the Kern. They read: *Do NOT go in the water!*

Thirteen drowning deaths this year. EXTREMELY DANGEROUS!

I guess those signs just weren't clear enough even though our original idea was to just relax by the cool of the river and get in some fishing.

After we arrived at a nice, calm spot on the river we set up camp, cracked a beer and tossed in our fishing lines. The fishing was terrible. We got completely skunked. We tried fishing from a four-man life raft I had brought. We anchored the raft out in the river with a rock tied to a length of nylon rope but still, no action.

I said to Jeff, "Hey Jeff, wanna switch things up a bit and have some real fun?" as I motioned down the river. Jeff smiled and looked back at me. We tossed our poles back on the shore and got two wooden oars I had brought along. I removed our rock anchor from the rope and we were off!

We instantly began moving at an incredibly fast pace. We each had an oar and immediately began figuring out how to use them to keep the raft straight. The term "backwater" began to be used (rowing backwards) to slow us down as we neared the first set of rapids. I immediately realized we were about to do something really stupid. No lifejackets, no safety equipment, no thinking, just spur-of-the-moment mental madness. The Kern had us in its current and we were at its mercy. I felt like I was in *The Proteus* in *Fantastic Voyage.* We had been injected into the bloodstream of this river and were being held, encapsulated in our tiny raft.

The Kern has its own dynamics—still glassy areas of water that then lead into churning rapids that crash into huge rocks causing a deafening sound then back into glassy stillness again. It's a truly beautiful, but deadly river.

Jeff and I could hear a rumbling up ahead. "Backwater!" I yelled, "Jeff, BACKWATER!" This was it. There was no turning back as we launched downwards into this water roller coaster as a handful of empty Coors cans went flying out of the raft.

There are not too many things that can compare with the excitement of whitewater rafting (Okay, I can think of a couple). But this was up there with the best of any experiences I ever had up to this point in my life.

Suddenly, in the middle of this frenzied ride, the raft suddenly stopped. It was pulled down several feet as roaring walls of water rose up on either side of us. I couldn't see what was holding us back. Looking all around the raft, I finally I saw it—the nylon rope had fallen out of the raft and vanished upstream into the rapids. The knot that had held the rock had undoubtedly gotten caught between two rocks thirty some-odd feet upstream.

"There!" I pointed at it. We tried to untie it at the boat but there were thousands of pounds of pressure on it and we had no knife to cut it with either. "I'll go and try to get it loose!" I said, "but don't let go of the line, and reel me in when it slacks!" Jeff nodded as I crawled out of the raft into the roaring Kern River.

As I pulled myself upstream on the nylon rope against the thrashing current, I didn't have a concern in my head. I was now out of the raft, no lifejacket on, and moving against thousands of gallons of water.

I reached the place where the rope was caught. I could see where the knot was gripped around a large rock. I crawled onto the large rock and looked back at Jeff giving thumbs up. I then carefully and slowly peeled the rope backwards over the large rock, knowing that the second it was free, I would be on the move. So I held on to it tight. Suddenly it was free and so was I, sending me hurling downstream as I held on to this literal lifeline.

Keeping my legs up in the air, I rode on my butt over several rocks in the rapids while Jeff reeled me into the raft and saved my life. Head over heels I tumbled into the raft, uprighted myself and down we shot into the white turbulence. Out of this hell, we found ourselves back in calm waters again drifting quietly downstream like two mice soaking wet. Jeff and I fell back, exhausted and trying to catch our breath, which was then followed by uncontrollable laughter.

As we drifted by campers on the shore, they pointed at us as if to say, *look at those fucking lunatics.* I can't put my finger on it but there's something really funny about almost dying.

Then came that distant roar again. We bolted upright at the ready.

"Backwater, Jeff." I said. We could see the rapids ahead now and there was a strange edge to them followed by a steamy mist. There was a drop! The closer we got, the more we could define what we had to do to maneuver. Several large rocks spotted the edge of the falls leaving few choices for, what looked like, narrow passageways for our raft to get through. I urged Jeff to try to keep the back of the raft upstream so we could shoot straight down without incident. But just then, the rear of the raft began to swing around sideways. We were headed for the falls sideways and would surely flip over.

We desperately tried to correct ourselves but it was too late. The raft began to slide sideways over the falls but then a rock stopped us midway directly at the center of the raft. The water crashed over us as we were hung up on the rock, flanked by two other large rocks on either side of us. The sound of the water was so deafening, we had to yell at the top of our lungs to hear each other. We were stuck. We devised a plan to plant the oars on the flanking rocks, and then on *three* to each give a mighty push, which theoretically, would pivot us around and straighten us out again.

It worked! We launched downward disappearing into the green foam. We found ourselves deposited into calm waters again as our tiny raft rotated out of this lethal, white-water washing machine.

Almost lifeless, we pulled ourselves ashore and deflated the raft, found the main road, extended our thumbs and the first passing car picked us up and took us back to our campsite.

We shot five miles of the Kern River rapids without lifejackets and somehow lived to tell about it. "We beat it!" Jeff said excitedly.

I slowly turned and looked at him, and in a husky voice quoted the words Burt Reynolds used in the movie *Deliverance*. "Nobody beats this river."

Chapter 16
Coyote vs. Chihuahua

Several memorable experiences happened to me when I was about sixteen or so. I lived with my dad up in the hills off Mulholland Drive. Remember where I scared the two women? There were no fences or landscaping or really anything that might determine property boundaries. Grass hadn't even been planted in many of these developments yet.

Our house was at the end of the neighborhood that was built along a hillside. A long concrete irrigation gully followed the hillside across the housing track and seemed to stop at our backyard. In the early morning hours, we could often see wild coyotes cross our backyard from having traversed the hillside along the cement gully. That sets the stage.

It was a hot summer night, as there are so many of, in the San Fernando Valley. I often escaped the heat by slumbering outdoors in my backyard in a sleeping bag. My Dad was often on location and I was often alone.

At the time, we had two pure white Chihuahuas named *Winky* and *Tinky*. (Again, I didn't name them.) They were these very small, shorthaired dogs that had very pale pink skin. It was like having puppies all the time but they were full-grown dogs. When I slept in my sleeping bag, they usually joined me by crawling all the way down to the bottom to sleep with me. And sometimes they snuck their way in after I had gone to sleep without me even knowing it.

Winky, Tinky and me.

On a side story, I remember Winky doing this. In the morning, I got up, rolled my sleeping bag up and put it away in the closet. Later that afternoon when I went to feed her and Tink, I wondered why she didn't come when I called her. Come to think of it, I hadn't seen her all day. I called her over and over. I tried to trace back to when was the last time I had seen her but couldn't remember. Then it hit me, *Oh no! Could it be? The sleeping bag!*

I quickly ran to the closet where my sleeping bag was, got it out and as I unrolled it I could feel something in there. I shuddered to think of finding her in there suffocated—or maybe it was just a cast off pair of socks. There I found Winky, still sound asleep at the bottom of the sleeping bag. She got up, stretched and gave a shiver, then trotted off down the hall to get a drink. Any other dog would have been freaked out or dead, I think.

Back to my story—I was in the backyard sleeping in my sleeping bag. In case of a coyote encounter, I brought a large kitchen knife with me and kept it under me.

In the middle of the night the sound of barking woke me up. I looked up and in the cool pale moonlight, I could see Winky and Tinky confronting a wild coyote. The hair on the coyote's back was standing straight up. At first I thought, "What's that coyote afraid of?" But the real danger was in the tone of the Chihuahuas barking. Just as my eyes adjusted to the darkness, the coyote grabbed Wink in its mouth and took off back down the drain gutter. I jumped to my feet and yelled, "NOOOOO!" I grabbed the kitchen knife under my sleeping bag and gave chase. I was wearing only my tighty-whities.

The concrete drain gully I was running down was v-shaped. It had a very rough unfinished concrete surface. I was in a full-on sprint. Just as I was gaining on the canine thief, I hit a metal irrigation pipe with my ankle, which sent me face down onto the unfinished concrete which acted like a cheese grater on my bare skin. But all I could think of was saving Winky. I got to my feet again, trying to regain the ground I had lost. By the time I was closing in again, I hit another irrigation pipe with my shin and went down again. It was a miracle I didn't land on the kitchen knife either time. Adrenaline surged through my veins like the current of the Kern River. But I kept my focus on getting Winky back. I uprighted myself again and rounded the corner of the hillside only to find the coyote facing me in a standoff position. There was no sight of Wink anywhere. The hair on the coyote's back was standing up but this time it was snarling at *me*.

Thank God the knife I was wielding was a large one. It gave me courage. If we were going to mix it up, I was intent upon doing my share of damage. A split-second passed. A million thoughts went through my head. Like, *man versus beast. No one knows I'm out here. What if it wins? Hey, I'm in my underwear.*

With a lunge, I let out a loud attack shriek. This spooked the coyote, making it turn and run off into the night and it was gone. It was over. I had won and no blood was spilled. I felt like a Viking that had just downed a Woolly Mammoth. But then, a much smaller animal returned to my thoughts: Winky. I turned and backtracked back down the gully and found her, lying there on the concrete. She was alive and, oddly, there was no sign of blood anywhere. I did notice she had several puncture wounds in her sides. "Oh, Wink. I'm so sorry, pup." I said stroking the top of her head. She slowly blinked and I knew she was going to be okay. I carefully picked her up in my arms. She opened an eye, saw me and seemed so grateful that I had her.

Cradling her in my arms, I gently carried her back to the house and wrapped her in a blanket. I called the emergency vet on Topanga Canyon and they said to bring her down right away. I had just gotten my driver's license and I grabbed my car keys. I threw on some white pants I had nearby and carefully sat her on the passenger seat. I got her situated and got in. She was so quiet I thought maybe she was dead. But I talked to her all the way to the vet.

When I arrived, the vet took one look at the dog and then looked at me and said, "The dog will be fine but you look like hell."

I was bleeding from everywhere. My white pants were red with blood from the knees down. My hands, wrists, elbows, tops of my feet and shoulders were raw and bleeding, too. The vet gave Winky a shot, then cleaned out all my wounds and bandaged me up. He told me to leave her overnight and that she would recover just fine and she did.

I saved my dog's life that night and the vet called me a hero. But the real hero was a 2-pound Chihuahua, named Winky, who took on a wild coyote and lived to bark about it.

Chapter 17

Mob Artist

A few weeks after graduating Taft High School in Woodland Hills, California, I was very lucky to get a job at NBC TV in the graphic arts department. I had started a successful band at Taft High School with a good friend, Randy Gornel, called Lil' Elmo & the Cosmos, and they were going great guns. We even had a single that was being played on KRLA radio that I co-wrote and were touring the Valley playing concerts.

But shortly after my graduation in '73 I was asked to do a sweet-sixteen poster for my friend Sue Firestone's little sister. Her name was Judy and she was on the Drill Team at Taft. So I did this caricature of her with her pom-poms, all hand-lettered and illustrated in full-color. Well, her Dad, Bob Firestone, flipped when he saw the poster of his daughter and asked, "Who did this?"

At that moment, my life changed forever. Bob was the accountant at NBC and said they needed summer vacation replacements in the graphics department and asked if I would be interested. My high school portfolio was a joke—many drawings were on lined notebook paper and lacked any sign of a professional artist. But there must have been something there (or they were just desperate) because it landed me a TV network gig at the tender age of eighteen.

Realizing I was not cut out to be a musician, I told the guys in the band good luck, (besides they needed a real drummer) and I decided to take a cue from the universe and pursue a career as an artist, instead. The term "starving artist" never really applied to me and to this day I am so thankful for that. I blew off going to college and went to work at NBC TV. Besides, I had always heard that on-the-job experience was better than any college training you could ever have. Several years later, I did take some night classes at Art Center. But looking back on it now, I don't think anything could have ever prepared me for drawing mob figures undercover at the Bistro restaurant in Beverly Hills!

My job at NBC morphed into me doing courtroom illustration assignments several days a week for the KNBC News Department. My first case was Leslie Van Houten's re-trial from the Manson murders. Courtroom illustrators have to draw very fast and many times capture the perfect moment in their head and then finish it in their mind's eye because everyone keeps MOVING! And a news crew is breathing down your neck while you're finishing it, waiting to film your art and broadcast it on the air LIVE! No pressure. Geez! Needless to say, I was very nervous and Leslie's detailed testimony of how she murdered the LaBiancas was a bit distracting, to say the least.

When Leslie Van Houten was questioned about the murders, she went into extreme detail. Trying to get a good likeness of her while she was recalling her murderous assault was something I'll never forget. She was cool, calm and almost enjoying the retelling of it, offering chilling details throughout. My color illustrations of her didn't hold a candle to the color she brought to her macabre retelling of murders so grizzly, it's no wonder she'll probably never see freedom.

I made it through the day but the drawings sucked. I figured that was it for my big foray as a courtroom illustrator, but they kept calling me back. I got better over the years as I learned the ropes.

Some of the trials I did included the Marvin vs. Marvin palimony trial, Sal Mineo's murder trial, the Hillside Strangler Murder trial, and many others. I've done a lot of crazy things in my life as an artist. I was the official UFO Sketch Artist for the TV show, *Sightings*. I listened to abductees' testimony describing aliens, probes, and their ships and provided detailed, on-camera drawings for many episodes. That was weird. I've worked with the police department creating police sketches for murder crimes and location renderings for famous directors. I even illustrated Bob Hope's Christmas card. I've been on one of Oprah Winfrey's shows doing graphic design on camera, and re-created near plane crashes with illustration for the news. But the most bizarre thing I ever did was when I was hired as an undercover sketch artist for KNBC News.

This is that story. (Deep breath) So, my boss at NBC graphic arts department, Art Trugman, the greatest guy in the world, comes to me mid-morning and says, "Mike, there are two network news reporters in from New York doing a story on some mob guy that's come out of hiding after thirty-five years—they need an artist today to draw him at the Bistro restaurant in Beverly Hills—undercover." After I picked up my jaw, I asked, "How?" I had on my usual attire, torn jeans and a t-shirt with tennis shoes. He told me they were expecting me in wardrobe and that I was to be fitted for a suit.

After taking my measurements in the wardrobe department, I was instructed to go to the art supply and get a sketchbook that didn't look like a sketchbook. I found this black, leather-bound book with blank pages that was perfect and returned to the studio.

Back in wardrobe, they fitted me in a beautiful three-piece, pinstriped suit. I looked like a million bucks. (Too bad I had to return it.) Then Art instructed me to go down to News and that they would have a brand new Monte Carlo with a two-way radio in it, waiting for me. This was getting better by the minute. I almost expected some guy named "Q" to explain some cool, hip weapons for me to carry. I was told to meet some bald guy named "Ira" in the *31 Flavors* on Rodeo Drive across from *The Bistro* restaurant at one o'clock. So I took off with my leather-bound sketchpad, dressed to the nines in my Monte Carlo with a two-way radio on my mission impossible.

At one o'clock on the dot, a guy poked his bald head into the door and looked at me and asked, "Mike?"

I answered, "Yeah," and the game was afoot. Ira and I walked about 300 yards down Rodeo Drive where I met the other reporter. There was also a beautiful woman with them, an airline stewardess, who I found out later, was there just to lighten the picture. Okay, makes sense. Now, I'm thinking, wait, this could be dangerous. What the hell am I doing?

These guys are just trying to get a story. I'm thinking, dude, this qualifies as putting yourself in harm's way.

I start looking around for police or, I don't know, maybe NBC security or a page or something. Nada. Nothing. There was just us, doing something very dangerous. Ira said he was going in to check on our reservation. He looks down the street about 300 yards at a white van parked there and says, "Frank, I'll let you know if anything changes." The headlights on this van go off and on.

This guy's wired for sound! Holy shit. What the hell have I gotten myself into?! I was sure my new found title as "undercover artist" was going to be short-lived because within an hour I was going to be dead!

It was much to my relief that Ira came back and said that the mob guy was not there. We would all meet back tomorrow, same time, same channel. Great, now I had twenty-four more hours to stress about how I was going to die at the hands of the mob. Terrific. My mind went to some very dark places and needless to say, sleep was not in the cards for me that night.

The next day I came to work, got in my costume and drove down to the ice-cream shop while I played with the two-way radio in the Monte Carlo.

"*Broad Sword* to *Danny Boy*—come in, *Danny Boy*." The guy at the news desk didn't think it was funny and told me not to mess around again with the network field equipment. My energy was up. Anxiety and fear had taken a temporary back seat. I checked myself in the rearview. Yeah, looking good, I thought. I was getting used to this undercover artist bit. I began to Walter Mitty out, thinking that NBC should do a pilot on me. I began doing the announcer's voice-over, "Tonight, don't miss the series premiere of *The Undercover Artist*. Armed only with his wits and a sketchpad, he's going up against the mob. Will he be able to draw himself out of this one? Tune in tonight after a very important, *Chico and the Man* on NBC."

Back in reality, I met with the group and they checked in with the restaurant to see if he was there. He was. It was on.

Apparently, this mob guy had gone into hiding some thirty years prior and dropped off the map. He was responsible for a lot of deaths and was now doing business with a group of businessmen in public at *The Bistro*. The reporters had a film crew inside the van who had captured him coming and going into the restaurant but they needed a few sketches of him actually doing business in the restaurant to finish their news story and that's where I came in.

Our table was about thirty-five feet away from the mob guy and his cronies. I could easily see him which also meant he could easily see me. I kept my cool and began to draw. We ordered lunch and had some light conversation although it was hard to resist the urge to run and scream at the top of my lungs while urinating all over myself. The thought of what I was doing kept going through my mind. I'm drawing a deadly mob guy undercover for the news! How ludicrous this whole situation was. If we all don't wind up on the front page of the *National Enquirer* it'll be a miracle, or even in the obituaries for that matter.

The reporters wanted two drawings—one tight shot of the mob guy showing his likeness and a wide shot showing the whole group at the table. I finished the tight shot and discreetly showed the reporters who both approved. I was halfway through. Phew.

I started the second drawing. I was feeling a bit more confident now that I would get out of there alive and relaxed into the moment taking more risky looks over to the table and for longer periods to study the group. Several telephones were at their table. Contracts were being passed around. They were obviously doing business.

The second drawing was almost complete when I looked over at the mob guy and he was looking directly back at ME!

"Shit," I said.

"What?" Ira asked.

"He sees me, he SEES me!" I continued under my breath. That was the first time I saw fear in Ira's eyes. If he had hair it would have been standing up straight, I guarantee you.

He told me not to look over there and to just have a few bites of my lunch. Sadly, if push came to shove, the Chicken Piccata and my pencil was all I had to defend myself with. Thoughts of flinging my plate, like Bond's Oddjob, across the room, played out in my mind. All I did know is that we were screwed.

I let two minutes or so go by and casually looked up like a nervous Woody Allen trying to be cool. The mob guy rose to his feet and pointed at me from across the room, then he said something to his group at the table. All of the businessmen got up and exited the restaurant at once. I turned white as I felt the blood drain from my face. Ira and the other guy got to their feet and threw a C-note at me saying, "If we're not back in fifteen minutes pay for this and go back to the network and finish." (Back then a hundred bucks would easily cover lunch for four at *The Bistro*) When I asked them what they were going to do, he said they were going to try to interview him now that he had seen us. This I found odd but by this time I had stopped thinking because I was completely numb with fear. My hands were sweating and my fingers trembled. I was not cut out for this James Bond stuff and I wanted to flee and leave the girl with the bill to pay. But I hung in and made some light conversation.

"So, what's your sign?" I asked her. We exchanged questions about one another as if none of this was happening—so weird. I wondered if she was as freaked out as I was. But then again, being an airline stewardess, she was probably used to the idea that when your time's up, it's up.

About ten minutes later, Ira came rushing in all disheveled and said to me, "Did you pay the bill?!"

"Not yet," I said. Ira, now showing his true state of mind, screamed across the fancy restaurant "Garçon!!" Everyone looked at us wondering what was so urgent. I asked him what happened and he said the mob guy got very upset.

In a high-pitched, falsetto voice, I said, "He did?"

"Yes," Ira replied, "And I'd feel a lot better if we all get out of here as fast as possible."

Oh, good, I thought, even this guy knows we could get killed. While we waited for the waiter to settle our tab, it seemed like forever. Wait-a-minute, who the hell cares about the change? I was outta there.

I fast-walked to my Monte Carlo. There I was, in plain view, an artist with a price on his head. I got in the car as I glanced back over my shoulder to see if anyone was following me. I had my eyes glued to my rearview mirror all the way back to the network expecting to take a bullet at any time. The upside is that if I was going to die, at least I would have looked good. I can imagine the cops saying, "Nice suit, cool car, too bad about the bullet in the back of his head."

Back at NBC I finished up the drawings, returned the suit to wardrobe and went home and had an anxiety attack on the floor. Just another day at the office.

Chapter 18

Magic!

My earliest memory of being introduced to magic was when my dad returned home after having been gone for six months working on *Hatari* in Africa. He arrived home with a large white box from *Burt Wheeler's Magic Shop* on Hollywood Boulevard. It was a deluxe magic set. Now this was not a present for my brother or me. My dad had bought this for himself! Here's this six-foot-four badass stuntman who just returned from hunting the most dangerous animals in the world and what does he do? He buys himself *Dr. Wizard's Magic Box of Tricks*.

If I was smart I would have threatened to tell his stunt buddies about it and he probably would have given it to me to save himself the embarrassment. But I was not smart, I was six. I was also the best audience in the whole house because he could trick me with no problem whatsoever. I was amazed at all of his tricks and the box filled me with a sense of wonder like no other thing I could have ever imagined. This box was the gateway to all of life's greatest mysteries as far as I was concerned. It held the secrets to the whole world and the higher up the shelf he hid it from me, the more I wanted it.

My father's tricks tortured me. There was this "India Vase" that poured a seemingly unending amount of water. My dad made up an entire story about a tribe of thirsty soldiers who were traversing the Sahara Desert with no water left and only this magic man among them to produce water with the wave of his hand whenever they needed a drink.

He would also place two little, blue, foam rabbits in my closed hand that would make babies and multiply magically. There were the Linking Rings, a rope that would magically get as rigid as a stick, the Hindu Coins and, best of all, was Georgie, the ghost who lived in a handkerchief! Georgie would rise up by himself and somehow vanish into thin air when my dad lifted the handkerchief up! This tore my brain out. I wanted to know the secret so bad it actually hurt my head to think about it.

There had to be a law against such child abuse. I remember going into my dad's bathroom while he was taking a bath and begging him for a peek inside the box. He finally looked me in the eye and said, "You really want it that bad?

I said "YES!" with resounding confidence. I'll never forget this moment; he looked at me and slowly smiled and said, "Okay, I'll sell it to you." I thought, *What?? Sell it to me?* I hardly knew what money was. The concept of money was so strange and completely unfamiliar to me. He wanted ten bucks for it. It might as well have been a million dollars. It seemed so unattainable and futile that my hopes and dreams were dashed to pieces.

I left the steamed up bathroom dejected and sweaty but not before my dad did another mind-blowing magic trick for me from the bathtub. And, by the way, "Who takes magic tricks with them to take a bath?" I thought.

But strangely after that, I seemed to be offered a dollar here and a dollar there for chores around the house that I usually didn't get paid for. I started doing the math and it was actually adding up. Saving up ten bucks for the secrets of life started to make good sense to me. The closer I came to my goal, the more I wanted to help out around the house. I was a regular little workhorse.

It had caught on around our neighborhood that my dad could do magic. Our neighbors, Harold and Lorraine, had a daughter, Carol, who was turning sixteen and having a birthday party with all her friends over. On the spur of the moment, they invited dad to come over to entertain at the party. They didn't know he had been drinking while watching a football game and was pretty much in the bag.

He arrived with his magic box of tricks wearing a black cape. I came along for the ride to see him in action in front of a crowd. He did his usual tricks that, by now, I had pretty much seen a dozen times or so. The girls were all amazed and he was eating up all the attention he was getting. I think at that moment in time if you asked him if he wanted to go professional, he would have said yes.

But then he said he was going to hypnotize Carol. What? What was he doing? This wasn't part of his routine. At least not any routine I was ever privy to. Carol excitedly sat on the arm of her couch and my dad situated himself across from her. He borrowed a medallion on a long necklace from one of her girlfriends and began to swing it in front of her from side to side. He told her, "Keep your eyes on the medallion. Your eyes are getting very heavy. You're getting very sleepy." And sure enough, she seemed to really be going under. I was fascinated how quickly it all happened. Had my dad hidden some mysterious talent from me all these years? At that moment, I got my answer when Carol passed out and fell backwards off the arm of the couch and hit her head on the floor. Her friends screamed in shock. Her mother ran to her, yelling, "Oh my God, Carol! Are you okay, honey!?"

Carol was out cold and drooling like a wet fish. My dad desperately tried to laugh it off and back pedal out of the awkward situation. They got a bag of ice for Carol's head that was quickly developing a nasty lump on it. She groggily came to as my dad quickly packed up his magic tricks and took off, leaving behind looks of distain and confusion.

He had gone from hero to zero in a heartbeat and left without having cake. His magician days went up in smoke like flash paper. That was the day my dad gave up magic and passed the torch over to me. Yes! The magic box was finally mine. I still had to cough up the ten bucks, though.

The magic set consisted of the kind of tricks that if you read the instructions, anybody could do. There are basically three *areas* of magic. 1) Tricks anyone can do; 2) Tricks that involve dexterity skills, like sleight-of-hand or prestidigitation; and 3) real magic. (If you believe in that.) Real magic is that stuff you see in the movies—the dark forces. Whether it's real or not, I don't care to know because it usually involves opening a door that can never be closed again. No thanks. I did almost cross this line once but I'll get into that later.

The *kinds* of magic consist of *close-up* magic, *parlor* magic and *stage* magic, all involving different proximities to an audience.

When I was about seventeen, I was introduced to sleight-of-hand or close-up magic. For me, this was love at first sleight. I was six again. Michael Hutton, a friend from high school and the manager of *Lil' Elmo*, my band, offered me lessons and I was a sponge. I soaked up everything Michael would teach me and I began building a library of magic tricks. Coins, cards, ropes, and impromptu magic—I loved it all. In fact I still, to this day, carry several Kennedy half dollars with me and an East African copper coin and my color-changing knives. This type of magic takes tons of practice to pull off. Misdirection, patter and presentation all play an important part of close-up magic. Anyway, I became obsessed with it—annoyingly so. After I started working at NBC, everyone became a target for me to fool or perform to. There I met John Shrum, the Art Director for the *Tonight Show Starring Johnny Carson*. I did a lot of the art and graphics for *The Tonight Show*.

I got to know John quite well. John was instrumental in my magic journey as he was also affiliated with *The Magic Castle* in Hollywood. I was too young to become a member because you have to be at least twenty-one to join and I was only eighteen. John asked me to illustrate the poster for their annual *It's Magic!* show. *It's Magic!* is a big stage show held yearly by *The Magic Castle* and I was so honored to be asked to do it. All my posters currently hang in The Parlor of Prestidigitation at *The Magic Castle*, which I couldn't be more proud. This job became my gateway into the private club for magicians and their guests. By the time I was 21 I had done several posters for both John and Milt Larsen, the owner, and I bartered my way into a life membership that normally cost big bucks to attain. I was very lucky.

While I was at NBC, another Art Director named Ray Klausen approached me about doing magic at a huge $400-per-plate charity function at *The Beverly Hills Hotel* called *The Bagpiper's Ball*. He asked me to do it a year in advance so I couldn't say "Gee, wish I could but I'm busy on that date." So, I committed to doing it. All he originally needed was a roving magician to do close-up magic during dinner— no problem.

Then he came to me later and told me the theme for the evening was going to be Magic and would I be able to do a stage illusion. Well, stage magic never really appealed to me because there are so many ways to trick someone thirty feet away. The challenge for me is being right up in someone's grill and blowing their mind.

So, I had to find someone who did stage magic to help me out. There was this arrogant guy named Pat who worked at the local Magic shop and I asked him if he could help me out. He did stage magic and said he would but he wanted to get paid. I was doing this for free, as it was a charity event, but I got Pat paid as he wished.

We settled on Houdini's *Metamorphosis* as the illusion we would do. During rehearsals, Pat would lock me in handcuffs inside a tied sack, then lock me in this large trunk. He would then stand on the trunk and pull up a sheet covering both him and the trunk and on *three* I would pop up and lower the sheet, unlock the trunk and reveal Pat locked in cuffs inside the sack. That's what was *supposed* to happen, anyway.

My 50th anniversary poster for the "It's Magic!" show

We were to have two lovely female assistants on the night of the performance. Pat was to hand the key to the trunk to one of them and her job was to later give it to me so that I could unlock it, revealing Pat. During rehearsals, the assistants were not present, so Pat would just put the key in his vest pocket.

The night of the performance came and *The Beverly Hills Hotel* was packed. This was an elegant, black tie event with a full band and a lineup of top-notch entertainment kicking off with our magical illusion.

Pat and I successfully pulled off the close-up magic part of the evening roving around the dinner tables and performing with no problem. While guests dined I would do card and coin tricks, vanish cigarettes and produce half dollars from dinner rolls. It was a blast.

Then came the main attraction—the illusion. The lovely assistants joined us and Pat got on mic and began presenting the illusion to the audience. He locked me up in cuffs, put me in the sack, and then locked me away in the trunk. Through the muffled sounds of the trunk I could hear Pat charming the audience. Everything was going according to plan.

I was doing all the secret stuff I can't really discuss here or I would get tracked down by the members of the *Magic Castle* and really be locked away in a trunk. He handed the mic to one of the assistants, jumped up on top of the trunk, pulling up the sheet around him and said, "Ladies and Gentlemen, Houdini's Metamorphosis! One, two and three!" Pat ducked down and I popped up revealing Pat had vanished. The audience applauded and loved it. I grabbed the mic and looked to the assistant and asked, "Can I please have the key?" Bewildered, she answered,

"He didn't give me the key."

"Well," I said, "Maybe he gave it to the other assistant." I approached the other assistant and asked her the same question. She too, replied, "He didn't give me the key, either." There I was, in front of maybe a thousand people or so, waiting for me to open the trunk and reveal Pat. So I began to vamp.

"Wow, nobody has the key." I said. The audience laughed thinking it was all part of the show. Inside I was thinking, *WHAT THE HELL AM I GOING TO DO!?* Then, I remembered Pat putting the key in his vest pocket during rehearsals. So I approached the trunk and said,

"Let's see if Pat has the key." I put the mic to the trunk and the muffled sound of Pat's troubled voice could clearly be heard. "What the hell's going on?!" Again the audience laughed, thinking it was all part of the show. I replied, still vamping for the audience, "Well, Pat we're looking for the key. Is it in your vest pocket?" I pointed the mic at the trunk and then clearly audible came his reply, "OH MY GOD!" He put the key to the trunk in his pocket. The audience roared with laughter. Instantly, I realized this was the out I needed. I bowed and said, "Thank you very much!"

I quickly ran up to half a dozen large men near a front table and asked them to quickly get up and help me out. They all picked up the trunk with Pat inside and carried it off stage. Everyone thought it was part of the show.

When I opened the trunk backstage, Pat emerged with his arrogance now a bit more tempered. I just smiled at him and said, "Well done, Pat."

Michael Bayouth

In 1976 when I finally did turn 21, John Shrum arranged for me to visit *The Magic Castle* officially as a member. I had been there several times delivering my posters to Milt Larsen, but this was official.

I brought a date with me and she was duly impressed. We had dinner there and during our dining experience, a round, old magician approached our table. I immediately recognized him as the world-famous Albert Goshman. Now, in magic circles, Albert Goshman is to magic like Paul Newman is to movies—or salad.

He explained that John had sent him as a surprise for my maiden voyage to the *The Magic Castle*. He sat down at our table as I told my date how lucky we were to be graced by this master magician's presence. He proceeded to blow our minds with his famous salt and pepper shaker routine followed by a sponge ball routine that I have never forgotten to this day.

For years I had heard that *The Magic Castle* had the most extensive, private magic library in the world. But it was only available to regular members and I was an associate member. In the coming year I did another *It's Magic!* poster for Milt and was granted a regular membership in exchange for my artwork. The minute my status was changed and I got my new card I went to The Castle with one thing in mind; the library.

The reason why I wanted to visit the library so badly was because I had heard it contained a locked bookcase that housed books on real magic— the dark stuff that was taboo to dabble in according to most magician circles. But, I had to admit: this fascinated me to no end. I had to see if it was there. I didn't know what I would do if it was, but I had to find out for myself. I was just so thrilled to finally have access.

The castle is not only a private club for magicians and their guests but it's a formal club requiring suits and ties for men and gowns or evening dresses for ladies.

So there I was, dressed to the nines by myself in *The Magic Castle* private library. There were several large, round felt-top, padded tables for practicing tricks surrounded by bookcase after bookcase of magic books. The secrets were mine. I had come a long way since that white box of tricks I had bought from my dad for ten bucks when I was six.

I slowly scanned the huge antique bookcases. All eight volumes of Tarbell's books were there. The Stars of Magic, featuring the professor of magic, Dai Vernon, books on Houdini, The Royal Road to Card Magic, Modern Coin Magic, the works. You name it, they had it—even very old books on magic from all over the world.

My eyes fell upon an ornate, antique bookcase filled with old books. I approached it and found it locked. This must be it, I thought.

On the fourth floor in the Castle are the production offices. I asked an older woman there about the locked bookcase and if I could open it. She looked me up and down and then slowly said, "Okaaaay." She opened her top desk drawer and held up an old antique key. It seemed to sparkle in the light. She laid it carefully in my hand, looked at me and said,

"Please, don't forget to return it." I assured her I wouldn't.

I had it in my hand now. I was so close. My mind was reeling with wonder as to what I might find. I reentered the library with key in hand and slowly approached the bookcase. It had two ornate, beveled glass doors. I felt a bit clammy and wanted to loosen my tie. I did, and then slipped the key in, and turned it. It clicked and unlocked. I slowly opened the squeaky cabinet door. It smelled of dust and some other vague scent I couldn't pinpoint. This was the moment I had waited for. I figured I would pick a doozy since I had my freedom of choice. I found a book entitled, *Demonism and Spiritualism*.

I carefully pulled it out and walked it over to one of the tables there and sat down. I opened the book to the first page, which was blank. The next page carried a small block of copy on it that read: *If your interests do not solely lie in what you believe to be the content of these pages, do not go any further.* I stopped. These words were meant exactly for people like me. My throat was dry and I tried to swallow but couldn't. I slowly closed the book, put it back, locked up the bookcase and returned the key. I have never been up there again.

Now I know why the private magic library upstairs at *The Magic Castle* is private. Suffice it to say, I am just fine with a few card and coin tricks.

Chapter 19
Friday the 13th

My dad portrayed Jason Voorhees in *Friday the 13th: The Final Chapter*—part 4 of the feature film installments. Many die-hard fans say my dad was the scariest and most menacing of all the Jasons.

When my dad invited me to the set I knew this was going to be an experience to remember. It wasn't surprising that my dad had no idea who this Jason Voorhees character was. Nor was he familiar with the popularity of the *Friday the 13th* franchise. A cowboy stuntman knows about horses, chewing tobacco, how to make a punch look like a hit and not a miss, and, most importantly, how to stay alive. But playing a killer was now the order of the day and he was to play the most famous killer of all: Jason.

The fact was, that he was embarrassed to even take on the role, but the money was good and he needed the work. He agreed to take the part with the understanding he was going to be un-credited.

My dad likes to scare people, though. He had that going for him. In this way, the casting was dead on.

On the set, my dad didn't take the mask off during breaks or even meals. He ate off by himself and didn't talk to the cast or crew. I asked him "Why, Pop?"

He said, "I don't want them to know me. Let them think whatever they want. It bothers people not to know who you are sometimes when everybody else is so nice and friendly. That's who my character is, someone who makes you feel uneasy."

Sacrificing the camaraderie of making friends on the set didn't seem to bother him at all. It all factored into the actors having a real life fear of him that he knew would inevitability rub off on the big screen, and it did! In fact, *Friday the 13th: The Final Chapter* has been touted as the most terrifying installment of the series—maybe my dad's method was why.

He had to arrive at the set in the wee hours of the morning to start the make-up process. It took hours just to do his fingernails. Legendary make-up artist, Tom Savini, did my dad's make-up. In 1984, I was 29-years-old. I got to be the fly on the wall during the filming of several scenes including a major kill scene.

The script called for Jason to kill this character, Doug, while he was taking a shower. It went down as the goriest scene in the movie when Doug gets his face crushed in the shower. Jason's hand smashes the guy's head against the tile wall and kills him.

So, to achieve this, a fake shower was pulled together with a running-water fixture. The camera was positioned in the shower and focused on Tom Savini's amazing life-cast of the actor's head. This fake head was a work of art with an uncanny life-like resemblance to the actor. Tom had fashioned a huge syringe full of fake blood under the prosthetic head that would shoot blood into the head as my dad did his dirty work.

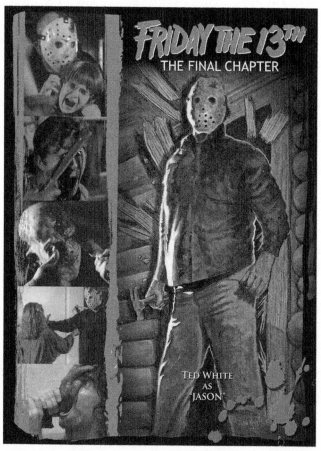

Illustrated for my dad as a collectible fan poster

Tom came up to my dad before the shot and said, "Now Ted, this is a very expensive prosthetic and we have to get several takes out of it—so take it easy on it, okay?"

My Dad answered, "No problem." Then the director, Joe Zito, came up to him and said, "Now Ted, this has got to be very visceral and violent so really give it your all. Don't hold back."

Again, my Dad responded, "No problem," and they rolled film. "ACTION!" yelled Joe. My dad's hand grabbed the head and began slamming it against the wall as Tom shot blood into the head. My dad's palm was logged in the head's mouth and blood began to flow out of the mouth and mix with the water making for a very gory effect.

"CUT!" yelled Joe and then took my dad aside. "Ted, I need much more violence. Really hit it hard. I want this to be very horrific." My dad assured the director he would, then Tom took my dad aside and said, "Ted, you have to be more careful with this prosthetic - it has to last for a few more takes."

"No worries," my dad said, "I'll be careful with it, Tom." I was cracking up listening to these two, very separate, yet parallel, private conversations—each of them being placated by my dad. A second take was shot. Both Joe and Tom again took my dad aside privately and each asked for much more, and much less, violence. Again my dad assured them he would give them what they were asking for.

But this time, I saw that look in my dad's eye when he assured the director and I knew this prosthetic was going to be history. Joe yelled *Action!* And my dad's hand began to violently smash Tom's work of art against the tile wall. Tom started yelling at my dad during the take to take it easy. But, in the true character of Jason, he was determined to kill this prosthetic head once and for all.

It was visceral. After the first two blows the head began to cave in from the pressure my dad was exerting. Hair was beginning to come out. Blood splattered everywhere. An eyeball popped out and dangled from the socket. Tom screamed, "TAKE IT EASY, TED!" My dad ignored Tom and continued his assault. I was amazed the set didn't give way. The head was flattened to a pulp. The jaw dislodged and hinged away from the skull. The director cheered and jumped up and down.

"CUT!" Joe yelled. "Print it, check the gate! Fantastic, Ted! We got it!"

Needless to say, Tom Savini's head didn't make it. There was nothing left but a pile of latex, plastic and hair soaked in fake blood.

I laughed all the way home that night remembering the experience. Another great moment in horror history.

Ted White as Jason from
"Friday the 13th The Final Chapter"

Chapter 20
The Christmas Special

It only takes one dope who thinks he can ski to ruin the whole shot.

I worked at CBS TV City for a while in the mid 80s as an Art Director for the Creative Entertainment Division. Occasionally, they would send me on location to art direct photography for ads for the CBS shows. This particular experience took me to Sun Valley, Idaho where CBS was shooting John Schneider for a Christmas Special. It was November and the ski season had not yet begun, although it had snowed recently and everything was blanketed in white power. This made for some great photography for the Christmas special.

The last night we were there called for a nighttime shot at the ski lift. A line of skiers with flares would wind down the hill in the background as John Schneider sang a classic Christmas song in the foreground.

Now, I love to ski and I had ski-fever, bad. I pulled some strings with the prop department and before I knew it I had a brand new pair of K2 Holiday skis, boots and poles and the clearance to be part of this nighttime mountain magic. I was stoked!

Four cameras had been allocated to capture this song in one take. As John sang, the effects crew would make it lightly snow on him and in the background a beautiful string of skiers with lit torches would snake down the hill. That was the *planned* shot anyway.

After I got all my gear on and I got to the chair lift I noticed all the skiers had a little logo on their jackets that read *Ski Patrol*. Huh, I thought, why did they get the ski patrol to do something so simple?

I was paired up with this guy and we were about to get on the chairlift when somebody grabbed my poles out of my hands and said,

"You won't be needing those. Here…" and handed me a flare instead. Nonchalantly I said, "I knew that, I knew that." At that moment, a twinge of panic surged through my body. I had never skied without poles before. We were whisked up the mountain. A moment passed as the reality set in of what I was getting myself into. I began to make some light conversation with the guy next to me. "So, how are the conditions on the hill?" In a calm, monotone voice he said, "Solid ice. The mountain hasn't been groomed all year. Season doesn't open until next week."

A high-pitched squeak slipped out of my mouth. He looked at me while my knees rattled and I just smiled at him confidently. He handily lit his flare so I followed suit but didn't know how to do it. I was pitiful. He had to light it for me. Suddenly, I felt like I was ten years old again. Fear had me in its grasp and I began to sweat in the below freezing night air.

Unlike the ski patrol members, I had never been trained to navigate on solid ice. The moment we disembarked the lift, I slipped on the grinding, rock ice and fell down. I was not cool. I got up and got in line with the skiers and waited for our cue from the patrol on the walkie-talkies. All four cameras began to roll and the director's voice could be heard through the radios saying, "Roll all four cameras, and, ACTION!" and we were off. Or, more accurately, *they* were off as I immediately fell down again and my flare went out. I panicked. *Oh, no*, I thought, *I don't want to ruin the shot if my flare is out. It will look like a string of Christmas tree lights with one light gone crazy!* Behind me, several ski patrol said, "Pick it up, pick it up." At this I said, thinking on my feet, or rather on my ass, "Go on ahead, I'll catch up." As the ski patrol skied off, I was so relieved that I had avoided ruining the shot only to realize it was suddenly getting very dark. The only light on that mountain was from those flares and mine was out! Now the fear of being left in the dark on that icy mountain had gripped me. I imagined someone finding me a week later up there frozen solid like a Popsicle.

I frantically struggled to get to my feet and catch up. The diminishing glow from the ski patrol's flares was becoming more and more faint. I had no poles to lift myself up. This was something I had never learned a technique for. As I tried to get up, I was all thumbs. The frozen ice cube I was on and gravity kept working against me. My body kept sliding away like an out-of-control hockey puck.

I finally managed to get on my skis again and I felt a sense of relief. Maybe I wouldn't die on that mountain after all. With arms outstretched, like one of the great

Wallendas walking a tightrope, I was quickly moving down, catching up with the ski patrol.

At this point I remember becoming aware that I was now probably also in the shot and needed to control my body with grace and style. This is where the difference of being an intermediate, recreational skier and a professionally trained ski patrol would also become painfully obvious. How to stop on solid ice is something they don't teach you in ski school on the bunny slopes. I guess the teachers figure that no one would ever be so stupid as to go up on an ungroomed mountain and try to ski on a solid block of ice. Well, they figured wrong.

I was moving at a pretty fast clip now and was quickly approaching the back of the line of the ski patrol. I tried to slow down by implementing the normally effective, and always trustworthy, snowplow technique. Nada, zilch, negative. I was about to slam into the back of the line of the ski patrol, which would have been very bad. I imagined all of the ski patrols going down like a line of dominoes creating the single most colossal fuck up in the history of television.

The only thing I could do was to fall down and let friction help slow me down. But, alas, even this plan was flawed as my splayed body, uncontrollably slid past them in a grossly unflattering manner.

In my mind I was imagining what the cameramen down below were recording at this very moment. John Schneider singing this tender Christmas classic while some buffoon up on the ski slope was spiraling out-of-control.

It happened several more times, getting back up only to catch up and fall back down again. It was, I think, the single most humiliating event in my life.

The crewmembers ribbed me about it for days telling me how it ruined the entire shot. I became the laughingstock of the set. Later they came clean and told me the truth. It was in fact, too dark to really discern my body flailing about on the mountainside.

Now, when I'm sitting around the fireplace at ski lodges, I just tell people, "Yep, I used to ski with the ski patrol," and leave it at that.

Michael Bayouth

Chapter 21
Stronger Than Dirt!

When my brother and I were pre-teens our family hung out a lot with Tom Sweet, another stunt man, and his family. He became known as the *Ajax White Knight* starring in a successful string of cleaning product commercials for Ajax cleaning cleanser. It featured him on a white stallion all dressed in armor with a lance that he'd use to point at dirty things and zap them clean. Tom and his wife, Jody, had two daughters, Karen and Kelly, that were close to the ages of my brother and me. We were all good friends and spent many evenings hanging out at each other's houses. We kids played games while the parents drank and shared stories of the stunt business.

In the West Valley, many homes offered horse property with stables in the back and, as I've said, stuntmen usually had horses. So, it was with Tom's house. Tom had a famous horse named Geronimo he kept in the back stables that had been used in many films. Geronimo was a red horse with four white socks and a blaze. He was the stallion in the *The Misfits* starring Clark Gable.

Ted White doubling for Clark Gable on location
during the filming of "The Misfits"

He had his own TV show called *Gallagher Goes West* and starred in *Son of Champion*. He had 125 cues on him that he never forgot till the day he died.

Geronimo chased my dad out of his corral once. Dad was giving him the cue to fight. Don't think my dad thought it would be that scary. He dove through the fence, drink in hand, and didn't spill a drop.

Morry & Margie Ogden, Tom & Jody Sweet & my Mom & Dad going to the Stuntmen's Ball

Center Ted's daughter Karen Rooney

One night at Tom's house, I remember the alcohol had been flowing, and my dad and Tom were pretty much in the bag. Tom was boasting how well trained Geronimo was, that he could come right through the house without ever getting spooked. Well, my dad took issue with this and a fifty-dollar bill was slapped down on the table. They shook hands and Tom left to go get Geronimo. My mom and Jody stopped talking and we kids got real quiet.

When Tom approached the back door with the large horse, Jody stood up and said, "Don't you even think for a moment of bringing that filthy animal into my house!" But the drunken cowboys had a bet and so in came Geronimo.

As Tom led Geronimo in, everyone held their breath. We kids grabbed up our game and stood back in shock. Here's this eleven hundred pound animal walking into the living room. The floorboards creaked under Jody's rustic braided oval rug. Chunks of manure and dirt were breaking off Geronimo's hooves and falling onto the floor. I'm sure Jody was having a hard time not throwing a tizzy fit, but she knew if Geronimo got spooked, it wouldn't take him but a few minutes to turn her beautiful ranch house into a pile of kindling.

Suddenly, it was as quiet as an operating room in there. Geronimo stopped. He looked around inspecting the interior almost as if he had a sense of design taste. I imagined him thinking, *Hmmm, so this is how they live?* My mom and Jody were exchanging incensed looks. This was not cool. They had gone too far this time and no one was laughing—yet.

Tom led Geronimo into the kitchen. They begin to circle the kitchen table. Dishes rattled in their cabinets. Geronimo's hooves left little good luck indentations in Jody's linoleum floor. I remembered feeling like someone was dismantling a bomb and didn't know which wire to cut.

Geronimo was brilliant—as cool as a cucumber. Tom was right. This horse was a one-of-a-kind animal. Tom clicked the air in his cheek and Geronimo followed him into the dining room and out the back patio doors. Back to the stable he went.

We kids were speechless. Tom returned, money exchanged hands and another drink was poured. The bet was over.

About a year after the Ajax White Knight commercials hit the airwaves, Tom took his white horse, Ajax, his armor and lance, a motor scooter and stuntman friend, Morry Ogden, on the road. The idea was to cash in on those Ajax commercials that were making Tom a household name. At first blush, the idea sounded good. According to my dad, Tom described it to Morry like this:

"We'll go to this huge rodeo coming up. There's gonna be sixty to seventy thousand people there. I'm gonna put ya on a motor-scooter, Morry. You're gonna be wearing all black, ya see. You'll come out doing about twenty-five miles-an-hour or so and I'll come out on my horse as the White Knight with my lance. I'll catch up with you and zap you with my lance and you'll have breakaway bungee cords on your dirty clothes which will all come flying off revealing you dressed all in white!"

It looked good on paper. Actually, back then, these ideas never really got as far as paper, I don't think. There was no real science to a lot of things stuntmen did back then. It usually started off with some guy saying, "I can do that," and a few minutes later that guy flying through the air and landing on his head.

So, all of Morry's dirty black clothes were set up to breakaway and come flying off. His clothes were fastened to these bungee cords that were connected to the back of the motor scooter. All Morry had to do when Tom pointed his lance at him, was to trip this switch with his thumb on the handlebar and his black clothes would come flying off. Presto, man in white!

They rehearsed the act several times—everything except the clothes coming off, that is. They were scheduled to come on right after the bull-riding event. An announcement over the loudspeaker introduced the Ajax White Knight as sixty thousand fans looked on. Morry came speeding out on his motor scooter. A moment later, Tom came galloping out on Ajax, as the White Knight. His armor outfit rattled and clanged as the crowd, who undoubtedly had seen the commercials, cheered and applauded.

They rounded the stadium once and on the second lap Tom caught up with Morry and gave him the zap, cueing for the special effect. Morry hit the switch on his handlebar and his black clothes came flying off. Well, some of them did anyway. One article of the black clothing covered Morry's head so he couldn't see a thing. Morry struggled to see but the force of the wind from the speed he was going, kept the clothing plastered to his face. It was too late. He and the scooter slammed head-on into the side of the stadium, pitching Morry about six feet up into the air and landing him smack-dab in the crowd. Morry continued wrestling with the black clothes still over his head, not realizing he had knocked a lady on her back with her feet sticking straight up in the air. Several other people and their chairs were upended as well.

Tom hollered, "Morry, are you hurt?" The up-side-down lady's husband said, "You crazy idiot, look at my wife. You nearly killed her!" to which Morry replied, "I didn't kill her!" The guy then said, "I'm not talkin' to you, numb-skull, I'm talkin' to the guy on the horse!"

Morry finally got himself back together. The motor scooter was completely bent up and mangled. Morry looked over at Tom and said, "This fucking deal is over with. I quit!" They loaded the demolished scooter into Tom's truck with Ajax, the horse, and argued all the way home. The Ajax White Night road show had started and ended all in one night.

Tom Sweet and his family rank amongst the fondest of my childhood memories. He was a wild, crazy cowboy who did some amazing things that I will never forget.

Like my dad and many other stuntmen, Tom Sweet was a giant. He had no fear of anything, I don't think. And that included flying.

Shortly after he earned his pilot's license, he was taking his family up north to visit relatives. They were flying a small Bonanza 4-seater over route 395 between the High Sierras and The White Mountains. Air currents coming down off the Sierras meeting the dry desert heat can cause some extreme updrafts. The Bonanza was caught in one of these and thrust out of control up into the clouds. Suddenly, in plain view, was all the detail of the side of the tree-lined mountain directly in front of them. It was too late. Tom had just enough time to pull back on the stick and pancaked the Bonanza into the mountainside.

When word reached us that they did not arrive at their destination, my dad was one of the first to get the call. Our family was on vigil for several days waiting for any kind of news at all. A snowstorm was hampering efforts for a rescue in that steep and rugged terrain.

The sad news finally trickled in more than 48 hours later. Tom and his youngest daughter, Kelly died in the crash. Tom's wife, Jody, and their older daughter, Karen, were in the back seat and, miraculously, had survived. This devastated all who knew and loved them.

Tom and Kelly will forever live on in my memory. Tom was a horseman, a husband, a father and a knight in shining armor. He was stronger that dirt.

Chapter 22
Roll 'em

The Universal back lot has many locations including a small western town. My dad and a handful of stunt guys, including veteran stuntman, Tap Canutt, were all playing cowboys in this modern day western. There was a large dirt hill next to this old western town. On the hill, was a dirt road that led down to the town where a big car rollover gag was being planned.

The stunt guys were all in between shots and thought they'd play a few rounds of Hearts. Over in the painter's department they grabbed one of several fold-up tables lying around and got the game going.

Art was the paint department head and I guess he was having a bad day. He stumbled upon the stunt guys playing cards on one of his tables and said,

"What are you guys doing with my table?" to which one of the stunt guys replied, "Just playin' cards."

"Well, we're gonna use *that* table" Art snapped. Tap pointed out that there were several other tables not being used. But Art was emphatic that they give up that specific table. The game was over. They shut the game down and left, murmuring under their breath, "That dirty, rotten son-of-a-bitch."

Later that afternoon, the car stunt was scheduled for Tap Canutt. The stunt called for him to turn over a 1923 Chevy 4-door sedan at the bottom of the big hill leading into town. Everybody wanted to get in that car to make money, but Tap got picked to do it. Tap sat in the car at the top of the hill, ready. It was the money-shot of the day. The car was idling as he waited for instructions from the director over the walkie talkie that sat beside him.

Art came walking by with a heavy five-gallon drum of paint. Tap looked at him and said, "Whadda got, Art?"

"I got paint." Art replied. Tap looked at the heavy drum in his hand and asked, "You gotta carry that all the way down the hill?"

"Yeah." Art said. "Why? You going down?"

"I sure am." Tap said. "You want a ride?" Art eagerly hopped in the sedan placing the five-gallon drum of red paint in the back.

Well, obviously Art didn't realize Tap was all safty-belted in, ready for a big stunt, or I think he would have opted out.

Over the radio chirped the director's voice *Tap, are you ready?* Tap replied in the affirimative, dropped the Chevy into gear and floored it. Down the hill they came. Art's eyes became as big a saucers. He yelled,

"What's going on!?" Tap just smiled and said,

"Hang on."

"NO! NO! NO!" Art shouted, quickly realizing he had become an unwilling participant in a car stunt—and with no seat belt on, to boot. But it was too late. Tap reached the bottom of the hill and yanked the steering wheel to the left. The Chevy rolled on a dime and flipped over like a poisioned cow. Inside the car, five gallons of red paint went in all directions. It covered everything including the both of them. Art was rolling around like a pea inside of a can.

After the stunt was over, Art had knots all over him. He was lucky he wasn't killed. Red paint was in his eyes, his hair, his mouth, everywhere. The stunt crew died laughing. Art may have had it coming, but I don't think he expected that.

The take was no good because the red paint killed the whole shot. Tap got fired from the picture but the message quickly spread throughout the union: *Painters, if stuntmen need a table, let 'em have it.*

Chapter 23
Wrong Is Right

Another great stuntman by the name of Dean Smith was on the set with my dad in *Wrong Is Right* starring Sean Connery. Dean overheard one the few conversations my dad ever had with the mega star.

My dad was to double Connery is a scene where he was supposed to be driving a Sand Sailor. Now, a Sand Sailor is a three-wheeled boat that drives on land. It has two wheels in the back and one on the front and a large sail on it. You guide them with a tiller like you would a boat. When the wind hits it, it will do up to eighty or ninety miles an hour.

So my dad is dressed like Connery's character and Sean walks up to him with two other guys. This is the conversation that Dean overheard.

Connery:	What's your name?
Ted:	Ted White.
Connery:	What are you going to be doing?
Ted:	I'm going to be driving your Sand Sailor for ya.
Connery:	Have you ever driven one?
Ted:	No.

Connery: Well, the script says he's going fifty-five to seventy-five miles and hour. You think you can do it?

Ted: If I didn't think I could do it, I'd call somebody else in here that could.

Connery: But you never even rode one of these things before. You know how to operate it?

Ted: I'm gonna learn in about five minutes.

Connery: What do you mean?

Ted: I'm gonna take it for a run.

Connery: What if you tear it up?

Ted: So what? They'll give me another one.

Connery looked at my dad for a moment then rubbed his chin.

Connery: You know what? I think you better go take those clothes off and give them to somebody who knows what they're doing.

Ted: You know what? Can I tell *you* something?

Connery: What's that?

Ted: Go fuck yourself!

~~~~~~~

In The Shadows of Giants

AFTERWORD

Well, that's it. Thanks for joining me for this collection of short stories. I hope you enjoyed them.

Looking back I try to imagine my life if it were different. I wonder what it would be like if I had grown up inside of another family—one that watched football together or took picnics by the lake or played miniature golf.

I remember being at home when I was a kid and I'd hear the front door slam and I knew my dad had arrived home. If it took him more than five minutes to walk from the front door to the family room where the rest of the family was, I knew it had been a bad day.

Taking risks was his job title. Like getting slammed into the bottom of a trash container from a giant scoop shovel in *Soylent Green.* Or holding onto the bumper of a car while getting dragged through a graveyard doing thirty miles an hour. Or maybe it was getting dragged off a cliff in nets in *Planet of the Apes.* I remember on *Ship of Fools,* with Lee Marvin, my dad had to get shot and fall off the mast of a ship while it was at sea. He had to fall just right through a hole in the deck of the boat and land on pads and boxes below in the hull. He spent hours up on that mast preparing for the stunt by dropping a ball at just the right time as the ship rocked trying to determine when it would fall through the hole just right. If he miscalculated it, he would hit the deck and it would all be over. There was a lot at stake.

Of course I can't compare the stuff I did in my life to him, but I look back and smile anyway. I have some great memories. And, although most of the stuff I did was not very thought through, I'm proud none-the-less and I wouldn't trade my memories for anything.

Kicking back on the sidelines and watching the action was never really my cup of tea. I had to get out there and get dirty. Be a participant. Caring what people thought was never really part of my filter system. Maybe it has to do with never losing that little kid mentality. I don't believe a young-at-heart mindset is only something you have when you're young. If you always do what they expect from you, you'll never surprise them. I think John Kennedy put it best when he said, *"There are risks and costs to action. But they are far less than the long-range risks of comfortable inaction."*

Now, when somebody asks me what it was like growing up in a Hollywood family, I could hand them this book and say, I grew up in the shadows of giants.

To view Michael Bayouth's portfolio visit:
www.bayouth.com

To view Ted White's fan website visit:
www.tedwhite.com

Other books by Michael Bayouth on Amazon
Nine Degrees North